Terry Waite has had a varied career and is best known as a hostage negotiator. He was also taken hostage himself in Beirut where he was kept in strict solitary confinement for almost five years. He has written about this experience in *Taken on Trust* (Hodder, 1993). He is also the author of *Footfalls in Memory* (Hodder, 1995) and two humorous books, *Travels with a Primate* (Hodder, 2000; Silvertail Books, 2014) and a comic novel, *The Voyage of the Golden Handshake* (Silvertail Books, 2015). His most recent book, *Out of the Silence: Memories, poems, reflections*, was published by SPCK in 2016. A co-founder of Hostage UK and Y Care International, he is also president of Emmaus UK.

Terry Waite

solitude

Memories

People

Places

First published in Great Britain in 2017

Society for Promoting Christian Knowledge
36 Causton Street
London SW1P 4ST
www.spck.org.uk

British Library Cataloguing-in-Publication Data
A catalogue record for this book is available from the British Library

ISBN 978–0–281–07881–3 (hardback)
ISBN 978–0–281–07882–0 (paperback)
eBook ISBN 978–0–281–07883–7

Typeset by Manila Typesetting Company
First printed in Great Britain by TJ International
Subsequently digitally printed in Great Britain

eBook by Manila Typesetting Company

Produced on paper from sustainable forests

Contents

First of all I must express my gratitude to the many people who agreed to talk with me when I was researching this book. Special thanks are due to Mark Lucas, who gave me all the contacts in Australia. Philip Law and all the team at SPCK were a delight to work with and were always helpful. Jenny Coles spent hours typing up my notes and putting them in presentable form. Thank you all.

Terry Waite
Suffolk 2017

Acknowledgements

A major part of the joy of serious travelling is in the preparation. The endless poring over maps and brochures, or researching on the internet, stimulates the desire to leave behind the day-to-day responsibilities and launch out into new experiences. I remember the excitement I felt as a child when my grandmother told me that she was going to take me on a day trip to the seaside. Having been brought up in post-war Britain, travel beyond the boundaries of the small Cheshire village where I lived was an exception. An exception that I welcomed with the same enthusiasm with which a prisoner might greet his impending release.

As soon as I gained a measure of independence, I began to travel beyond the shores of the British Isles. First to France, Germany and Austria in the days when it was safe and easy to hitch-hike across Europe. Later my work took me to Uganda, in East Africa, which eventually became my home for several years and also the birthplace of our youngest child. After Africa, the world opened to me. North and South America; the Middle and Far East; Australia and New Zealand. Sometimes I travelled in the company of others. More often than not I was alone.

Then, suddenly, my journeys came to an abrupt end. While seeking the release of hostages in Beirut I was taken captive and spent one thousand seven hundred and sixty-three days in captivity, almost four years of which were spent in solitary confinement. I have attempted to describe that experience elsewhere; suffice it to say here, it was during those years that I began to travel in my head. Using my imagination I crossed continents, sailed the oceans, and retreated into the inner recesses of my mind in order to try and understand myself more completely. On release, some five years later, I stayed put for a while in Trinity Hall, Cambridge writing my account of the experience. When the book was completed, I resumed so-called normal life once more. Having spent so much time in solitary confinement it was the solitary aspect of life that interested me.

1

In my book *Taken on Trust* I tell the story of my captivity and survival. The first edition of that book concluded as I stepped off the RAF plane in Lyneham, Wiltshire, and gave a press statement to the hundreds of journalists present on that wet and windy day. In a later edition I added another chapter, which briefly brought that book up to date.

This book picks up the story and recounts some of the journeys I made to solitary places and also records some of the people who spoke with me. They are indeed a diverse group, ranging from the wife of a cattle rancher living in the middle of the Australian outback to a former double agent settled in a government apartment in Moscow. They all spoke with me about solitude and how they viewed and lived it, and I have attempted to faithfully reproduce what they said to me.

In the final chapter I have added some further reflections taken from my own experience and, throughout, have included personal insights. There is no interview with any individual who has chosen a solitary life for religious reasons, and the exclusion is partly because there are so many writings about this experience that I did not feel the need to include more here.

Some years ago I read Anthony Storr's book *Solitude*, which is almost certainly the classic work on the subject. In it he quotes De Quincey, who said: 'No man will ever unfold the capacities of his own intellect who does not at least checker his life with solitude.'

Increasingly in today's frantic world we need space for ourselves. Recently a friend told me a poignant story which illustrated this point perfectly. He was leading a trek across a barren part of South Africa. For miles around, there was nothing but sand, sky and the wide open space. He noticed one man walking alone and, as he approached him, he saw that tears were streaming down his face. Anxiously he asked him if all was well.

'I've never experienced anything like this before,' he replied. 'My life is just full of the pressures of work and family. For as long as I can remember I have never experienced such beauty and peace in solitude.'

Perhaps this small volume may encourage someone to move fully into that space and explore more completely the richness of solitude.

Part 1

PLACES OF SOLITUDE

I feel a slight bump and open my eyes. We are passing through a patch of turbulence. The seat-belt sign illuminates and, automatically, I check that mine is secure. A steward passes through the cabin, sees I am awake, and asks if I need anything. I ask for a glass of sparkling water. Within a moment it is delivered complete with ice and lemon. 'Would you like a blanket, Mr Waite?'

I thank him and refuse his offer. He disappears through the curtain as my neighbour turns fitfully in his semi-conscious sleep. I sip my drink and leaf through the airline magazine. Maps fascinate me. I remember the time when my guard brought me an encyclopaedia – the letter M. I turned to the map of Maine and spent hours wandering, in my imagination, along the rugged and broken coastline. Now I examine the global map and in particular the map of Australia. According to Qantas, all roads lead eventually to Sydney. On the world map I look for Lebanon, my involuntary home for almost five years. There it is! A chunk of coastal land carved from the flank of Syria. It was there on the shores of the Mediterranean that I began to see the many faces of solitude.

A voice booms in the distance. I can't make out what is being said as there is a constant steady roaring in my ears. Lights begin to flicker and suddenly they explode before my eyes.

'Ladies and gentlemen. Shortly we will be landing in Bangkok. Please make sure that your safety-belt is securely fastened and your seat is in the upright position.'

As I awake from dozing I recognize the ritual formula repeated thousands of times daily the world over.

'Will you get out here for a while?' my neighbour questions me. He is ready to leave.

'I might stretch my legs. It's many years since I was in Bangkok.'

Like all proud citizens the world over he tells me how the city has changed. How the airport has developed. 'We have our problems, of course, but we are working on them.'

The doors are unlocked and there is the usual confusion as over-head lockers are emptied and the crew members endeavour to work out which exits will be used.

'Goodbye, sir; thank you. Goodbye, sir; thank you.'

The cabin staff dispense the final benediction before assembling their bags with telescopic handles and marching to their two-day sojourn in a downtown hotel room.

Before leaving the plane I attempt to remember the terminal building as I last knew it. It was quite small and there were no more than half a dozen shops. One sold inexpensive silk ties and scarves, another elephant leather wallets and luggage, and a third the ubiquitous duty-free spirits and perfume. Unsurprisingly a work of transformation has taken place. Now the corridor stretches endlessly to my left and right. The items on sale have multiplied a thousandfold. I take a bored, cursory glance at the emporia and set out to find the toilets, which, for some inexplicable reason, are hidden behind a maze of passageways. In the final departure lounge some five hundred travellers wait to board their plane.

'You are Mr Waite, aren't you?' A slightly built man with a pencil moustache stands by my side. 'I have read your book. How do you feel now? It must be strange to be with so many people.'

He asks the same question that thousands of people ask and I tell him that I am well. I don't tell him that I have changed. I don't tell him that while I don't find it difficult or object to being with large groups of people, I prefer the quiet of solitude. I don't tell him that this very day I am setting out on a pilgrimage to explore that very subject. I want to meet people whose experience is deeper and richer than my own. I want to know how they embraced solitude and if the embrace crushed them or if it brought a little joy, a little life to a fading mortal existence. I want to hear the different songs of solitude. I want to blend my voice with that great solitary cry of humanity that echoes and reverberates throughout the universe. To say all this would be impossibly pompous and tedious.

'I'm pleased you are well,' he continues. 'Many of us thought about you.'

I thank him again and he disappears into the crowd. Although there are times when I don't particularly welcome an intrusion, I confess to being moved by the genuine concern of so many. It's as though they are saying: how would I have coped? Would I have gone mad or would I have been able to find a life-bearing embrace from the experience? They ask some of the questions I continue to ask myself. How did I survive? What meaning can be found from solitude? Do I have a distinctive solitary song and at what point does that song merge into a great chorus?

The flight is called and we begin the slow shuffle past the desk clerk, the long march to the aircraft and the final squeeze into our seats. I am already into my pilgrimage. I am beginning to hear the first bars of a haunting melody.

*

Maps can be very economical with the truth. Admittedly, they do convey vital information for the navigator and professional traveller, but they can be misleading. I look at a name on a map – Mount Isa, for example – and immediately my imagination runs away with me.

We have been trekking all month across the parched earth of northern Australia. Our supplies are low. Suddenly in the distance we see a mountain peak. 'Isa!' we cry. Mount Isa. There are a few simple cabins, one general store, clean cool water . . . And so on.

Maps hold that sort of promise. The reality is often sadly different!

Isa is situated some four hundred miles east of Townsville and directly south of the Gulf of Carpentaria. Clustered around it, like supporting patrons at a charity ball, are such romantically named places as Duchess, Quamby, Ardmore, Georgina Downs and . . . Gunpowder. If the latter didn't set off warning bells, then Phosphate Hill ought to have done!

I had spent a restful weekend with friends in Sydney, sipping cool drinks on their sun deck overlooking the harbour. At Sunday lunch, when it was considered that my wits might have caught up with me from London, I was briefed. I was to travel by a commercial flight to Isa; there I would be met by a private plane from the Stanbroke Pastoral Company and after a brief stop at a cattle station in Cloncurry would head out across the Tanami Desert to visit the most remote roadhouse in Australia.

The first warning sign that my cartographical imaginings were about to be shattered became evident as we circled Isa in preparation for our final approach. For two or three hours we had flown through clear skies over the red barren scrubland that makes up so much of Queensland and the Northern Territory. I peered through the cabin window anxious for a first sight of the delights of this remote mountain hideaway. I saw a chimney. It was a very big chimney. It was belching forth smoke. Black smoke. Lots of it. There was a second chimney. Not quite so large, but equally productive.

We circled the town. A huge scar ran through the centre, suggesting that some serious extractive work had taken place and the operators had forgotten to suture the wound. I felt a surge of disappointment.

The plane touched down a mile or so from the chimneys. As I walked across to the terminal building, a notice proclaimed that the adjacent hangar was home to the Flying Doctor Service, or at least to some of their aeroplanes. Graeme and Neil from the Stanbroke Company were waiting for me in the terminal building. Graeme wore blue jeans, a bush shirt and a battered Stetson. He was a lean six-footer with an appealing grin, behind which lay a thoughtful and at times worried expression. Neil was shorter, stocky and hatless. They had the Beechcraft waiting on the tarmac but suggested that we take a quick trip into town to get some lunch and see the sights. Most prudent travellers had phoned ahead to reserve cabs, so we were left for a while until a spare vehicle came by. Eventually a car drew up and the driver gave us a broad smile. He had a distinctly Irish look about him, but his beer belly indicated that he was in fact a true Aussie. Graeme and Neil urged me to sit in the front and from the back told the driver that we wanted a tour of the town, after which he was to drop us at a place where we might get lunch. That was the only cue he needed. For the next hour he gave us a non-stop commentary.

'This is the greatest little town in Australia,' he said, as though he knew instinctively that he had to try and reassure me. We drove past the clutter and mess that distinguishes mining towns the world over. He pointed out the chimney.

'I took a greenie round some time ago. "Aren't you worried about the smoke?" he asked. "I'm bloody worried, mate," I said, "when there ain't no smoke. No smoke – no work."'

We remained silent, partly because we were pondering the remark and partly because we couldn't get a word in edgeways. When he paused for breath I seized the opportunity and expressed surprise that there was so much work for cabs in town.

'Look, mate, this car is worth two hundred and fifty thousand dollars. One quarter of a bloody million. That tells you something, eh?'

As he talked it became clear why he was so attached to Isa. Isa had given him a good living. He had worked hard in the mines for years, saved his money, bought a couple of houses and a cab, and never looked back. Graeme and Neil, both accustomed to living on remote cattle stations where there wasn't even a cab on a tractor, sat silently while our guide gave us his view on politics and politicians, and at the same time pointed out the sights. We drove past an ordinary-looking house where, according to our guide, the Queen and the Duke of Edinburgh had once stayed. Then we went to look at some flats. It all reminded me of tours conducted in East Germany in the sixties.

'I'll take you to the lookout,' he said. 'You'll get a fine view from up there.'

We drove up a modest hill and climbed out of the car to stare at one of those signposts that indicate the distance to Rome, New York, London and other exotic locations. Exotic, that is, unless you happen to live in them. There seemed to be nowhere posted that wasn't thousands of miles away. When we returned, our driver immediately started to talk again.

'Did you notice anything up there?' he asked.

'Yes,' I replied, taking the opportunity to pull his leg over his amazing ability to talk non-stop for well over an hour. 'It was much quieter.'

He gave a good-natured belly laugh and told us that he hoped we would have seen how green Mount Isa was becoming. There were patches of green where lawns had been carefully tended and I supposed that if you could forget about the mine and the smoke, and if Isa had been good to you and given you an opportunity in life, then it would be quite possible to think fondly of it. Neil, conscious that we had to fly that afternoon before the rains came, suggested that it might be time for lunch. Our driver recommended the Irish or the Buffalo club. Neither Graeme nor Neil were great club-men, although Graeme admitted that he might have been thrown out of the Irish club some years ago. We decided to play for safety and headed for the Buffalo. Here, somewhat reluctantly, we said farewell to our guide.

'It's a great little town,' he said, as he eased himself back into the cab. 'It's the greatest little town in Australia.'

One week later the following item appeared in the Isa-Spy column of the local newspaper, *The North West Star*:

> With rumors (*sic*) still rampant that low-profile author Salman Rushdie is hiding out in Mount Isa, the spy can now report that the city has played host to another international identity.
>
> Terry Waite, the American (*sic*) who was held hostage for two years (*sic*) in the Middle East by anti-US fanatics, made a flying visit to Isa earlier this week.
>
> He with two other blokes, flew in, took a cab ride around town and flew out again. Purpose of the visit is unknown. Maybe he was looking for Salman?

2 Constantine

Rain clouds were gathering as we clambered into the company plane. We had lunched on steak, chops and chips, and felt suitably contented. Graeme looked happy.

'Take a flip round the station, Neil. Let's look at a few of the waterholes.'

As Neil started the engine and exchanged unintelligible phrases with the control tower, Graeme explained that there had been a bad drought for the past several years. This year the rains were late, but it seemed as though now there would be some water at last. As Mount Isa receded into memory, Graeme plied me with facts. Hundreds of miles of fencing; thousands of head of cattle; millions of acres of red scrubland. Every quantity was enormous except when it came to human beings. A handful of people ran the ranch at Constantine where we were to spend the night.

'We're now over the property,' shouted Neil. 'Look, that creek's full.'

At the sight of water, Graeme's grin developed into a broad, excited smile. 'Bloody great,' he shouted. 'We need that, and more.'

Neil flew over the flat, red land.

'If the rains keep up, within a couple of weeks we could have grass waist high.'

It was hard to believe that the parched yellow scrub would ever flourish again. We flew onwards for mile after mile. Occasionally we would spot a few head of cattle, a borehole, a dusty track winding its way into the unknown distance.

'We'll put down in Cloncurry,' said Neil as he began to climb again. 'From there it's only half an hour by truck to the ranch. It's the last town you'll see for a long time.'

Cloncurry was a pleasing frontier town of five thousand inhabitants. Wide streets, a few shops, a couple of schools and a hospital with no doctor.

'They won't stay,' said Neil. 'They have to take care of the hospital, run a practice and be on call every bloody hour of the day and night. They come out here but soon pack up and go elsewhere.'

Cloncurry lazed in the afternoon sun. It reminded me of the sets especially built by movie-makers. At any moment I expected to see a posse of desperadoes hurtling down the main street, followed by half a dozen Graeme look-alikes. We drove around in the pickup, collected a few supplies and headed out of town. Soon the bitumen gave out and we bumped on to a dirt road. The red earth and parched scrub reminded me so much of Africa. Thirty years previously I had driven through such countryside in Uganda, Rwanda and Burundi. In Africa, for the first time in my life, I felt that I was in touch with the earth. The dust got into my hair and between my toes. Being in touch with elemental forces both excited and disturbed me.

Now, on the other side of the world, the same emotions stirred. This was a land still possessed by the spirits. By sheer determination European man had attempted to tame and contain. At intervals the spirits struck back with a fearsome hide-cracking drought or a super-abundance of rain that swept all before it. The survivors had entered into a respectful truce. Their faces, as burned and scored as the land that gave them their life, told the age-old story of suffering and survival. Aboriginal man, who once walked hand in hand with the spirits, now trod with uneasy, defiant step. In the city the spirits were entombed, buried beneath layers of concrete, their voices silenced. In the bush, like European man, only the strongest Aboriginal could survive. Only those who could remain totally in communion with the earth would be able to resist the debilitating forces that would reduce them into nothing more than shambling, dispossessed shadows. This was a hard, beautiful land.

*

'In all my years in Australia, I've never had a better time or warmer welcome. Thank you, Phylis and Bill, for your kindness to me and my party.'

So wrote the American ambassador to Australia on 24 June 1980. I was leafing through the visitors' book strategically placed in the guest room at Constantine. A visitor from the British High Commission had left his name without any message. He disappointed me, although I was impressed by his neat handwriting. The last entry was some two months ago: 'Here for the challenge,' wrote the guest.

I couldn't resist capping this by inscribing my name and including, 'Here for the beer.'

'You'll start a trend,' said Graeme's wife Sue, as we chatted in the kitchen. 'We do get visitors from time to time. Foreigners think this is a remote place, but it's not at all. It's so near to the town that the Flying Doctor Service don't come out, although they will give advice over the phone.'

Sue was a large, jolly woman in her middle thirties. She ran her domain with efficient good humour. Her story was not an unfamiliar one. She had been a governess. That quaint Victorian designation is still given to those who are engaged to educate station children. She met and eventually married Graeme and they settled on the Constantine station. As a senior inspector for the company, Graeme had to travel to many different stations, but he admitted that he preferred to live in a more remote location.

'I don't know why that is,' he said. 'I just like it out in the bush. This is the nearest I've lived to a town for years.'

Sue laid out supper in the front room. As we ate, the rain began to fall. Again, sitting in a bungalow with the rain bouncing off the iron roof, I was reminded of Africa, especially when the mains electricity failed. Graeme didn't even move, as a standby generator automatically swung into action. I told them how thieves in Uganda, protected by the noise of the downpour, would attack during a storm. Thieves were not a problem for Graeme and Sue. They had known the odd animal to be butchered, but there was nothing serious.

The rain continued while the frogs barked joyously throughout the compound. We were sleepy. Soon after nine we called it a day. I paddled my way, under cover of the eaves, to the guest room and unfolded my map. The following day I would leave with Neil for a journey into one of the most remote locations in Australia, Rabbit Flat, some several hundred miles away on the far side of the Tanami Desert. Before getting into bed I read a warning note on the map:

CAUTION

It is possible for conventional vehicles to travel the Tanami Track but it is only recommended for experienced travellers. High clearance vehicles are recommended. Much of the track is impassable in wet weather, supply of fuel cannot be guaranteed and heat can be extreme. Organise periodic contact with a friend who is aware of your travel arrangements. The Rabbit Flat road house is one of the most remote in Australia. It was pioneered by Bruce Farrands and his French wife Jacqueline in 1969 . . .

I was soon asleep. The sound of falling rain can be very soothing.

I sat next to Neil in the co-pilot's seat of the Beechcraft. He handed me a map and pointed out that we were to fly directly west. As he conducted the final departure check he told me that he had not flown this particular route before.

'There are rain clouds about. Once we are under way I'll climb to about eight thousand feet to get above them. With a bit of luck we should be there in about three hours.'

While we taxied along the runway, Neil asked me to hold the door open to keep the cabin cool. When he had lined up for take-off I slammed it shut and we were off. Within a matter of moments Cloncurry was behind us, and before us lay the wild open space that constitutes so much of the Northern Territory. Neil set the satellite navigation system.

'These things are bloody marvellous until a satellite goes down. Then it's back to the old map and compass. When they work they can get us to within a few feet of our destination.'

We were flying over an area so remote that it wasn't even named.

'What happens if there is an emergency and we have to put down here?' I asked somewhat nervously.

'Search and Rescue would find us . . . eventually.'

The radio crackled into life, but Neil told me that we were too far away to make contact with ground control.

'We may be able to get a message through via another plane. If not I'll phone them when we arrive. If I don't do that it'll be panic stations within a few hours.'

We climbed above the cloud cover.

'I did a bloody silly thing once,' said Neil, after he had locked on to the automatic pilot. 'I was coming in to land at Isa when suddenly there was the most god-awful racket. Then I knew – too bloody late. I had forgotten to lower the undercarriage. I've never lived it down, but we all make mistakes.'

That admission of human error endeared Neil to me. Many people would have kept such an event well under wraps, but Neil, in his direct, honest manner, was quite prepared to talk about it. I told him that I had a small favour to ask of him. When I was in captivity our youngest daughter, who was a student at the time, had gone with some friends to Australia. They got hold of a car and drove up the Stuart Highway to Darwin. Later that day we were due to pass over that very road and I wanted to see it. An hour or so later Neil brought the plane down below the cloud cover. The terrain had not changed since we left Cloncurry. Red earth, scrub, a few spindly trees. Suddenly we saw a dark, straight strip in the distance.

'That's it,' shouted Neil.

We came down low. Winding its way through this most remote of landscapes was the highway – totally deserted. I don't quite know why I felt so moved. Perhaps it was the thought that while I was laying in my prison cell attempting to plot my way through the inner pathways of solitude, my daughter was travelling through this wilderness. The road stretched endlessly below us, resolute in its purpose to reach Darwin on the Gulf of Carpentaria. Within moments it was behind us and we were over untamed land again.

It was early afternoon when Neil shouted across to me that, according to the satellite system, we should be over Rabbit Flat in a few moments. To the north-west I could see a small range of hills. There was no sign of habitation.

'See that track?' asked Neil. Beneath us there was a winding mark in the earth as though a child had dragged a stick through the sand. 'That's the Tanami Track. And if I'm not mistaken we should be over the house in two minutes.'

He was not mistaken. We could now see the property. There were just a couple of buildings with a pickup truck parked alongside. A few hundred yards away someone had sweated to clear and level the desert and forge an airstrip. A threadbare windsock flapped in the half-breeze. We circled the compound looking for signs of life.

'Perhaps they've gone to the supermarket,' quipped Neil. 'If so, they should be back in a fortnight.' He turned to me. 'You know,' he said, 'only a bloody crazy Englishman would come all this way for a cup of tea and a sandwich.'

*

It had taken me several days to reach the first true solitary situation of my journey, but that was somehow appropriate. It was in Beirut that I first met solitude face to face. Before that experience I had often been alone, but there were always other people around and, as and when I wished, I could seek their company. In captivity it was very different. For almost four years I was alone. The first encounter with my guards was intimidating and occasionally brutal. I was questioned and sometimes beaten. I had to learn how to control my imagination in order to prevent myself from becoming paralysed with fear. Eventually the questioning ceased and I was left alone. On odd occasions my guards would exchange a few words with me, but they were under strict orders not to talk to me. Each day, each month, each year, I was left alone with my thoughts. I discovered then that solitude needs to be approached gradually and experienced calmly. It is not just a matter of being quiet for an hour or so. Like a journey to a remote region, it takes a long time to reach the location and even longer to begin to appreciate the positive benefits of the experience.

As I stepped out of the plane at Rabbit Flat, I recognized that this wild, untamed territory represented in part an aspect of my own identity. Within me there were the remnants of an ancient aboriginal spirit. I recognized that spirit in captivity, when primitive emotions threatened to destroy me with their force and power, and also when those same emotions came to my aid to enable me to survive. It was impossible to bury them under the concrete of status or social respectability, because both had been stripped from me. Like the Aborigines of old who trod this very soil on which I was standing, and like the pioneers of yesterday whom I was about to meet, I had to be in touch with my instincts and learn how to trust them.

*

Now that the engine had been shut down, it was perfectly quiet. As Neil completed his paperwork, I climbed out and stood on the packed-earth airstrip. The nearest town to us was Alice Springs, some six hundred kilometres down the track. If we took the track, roughly fifty kilometres would see us at the Granites Mine, after which we would have an open run until we came to the Yuendumu Aboriginal Community at about the halfway point. Then there was not much else until the Tilmouth Roadhouse and, finally, Alice Springs, which is still considered to be somewhat remote.

Neil jumped down and joined me at the end of the airstrip. Nearby there was a solid iron girder to which was attached a length of chain.

'That's how they keep this strip in such good condition,' he said. 'They hitch the girder behind a truck and tow it up and down. It's very much cheaper than a grader and pretty effective. This is a very good strip.'

Suddenly the silence was broken and we heard the sound of a truck approaching. A battered jeep rattled into view and pulled up beside us. Behind the wheel sat a man with a full black beard and wearing an ancient Stetson. His eyes were just visible beneath the broad stained brim of his battered hat. They shone with good humour. He leaned out of the window.

'How are yer, Terry? I'd know yer face anywhere.'

That rather took me aback. I had become accustomed to being recognized in different parts of the world but I hardly expected it at Rabbit Flat.

'We followed yer troubles, mate. Bloody hell, what bastards there are in the world. My name's Bruce. Bruce Farrands.'

He leapt nimbly out of the cab and helped us put the luggage in the truck. The three of us then clambered into the front seat and bumped off down the track towards the house.

'My wife Jacqui's at home. Glynn is also here at the moment. He's my son. A twin. The other one is away in the military.'

We drove past two petrol pumps, vintage 1960. Attached to one of them was a notice: 'Please check price before filling up.' Good advice, I thought, although if you were low on fuel there were no other options. Bruce stopped in front of the house and let us out.

'I'll put the truck around the back. You go in.'

We entered into what appeared to be a communal dining room. In a corner was a serving hatch protected by a strong wire grille. Behind it were stocks of biscuits, chocolate and tinned goods. A young man appeared from behind the dry goods and gave us a rather surprised look, followed by a shy smile.

'Hold on, I'll let you in.'

We heard a key turn in the lock and the side door opened. We followed him down a small passageway into what was the family room. Outside I could hear the familiar hum of a diesel generator. All the windows were covered with curtains or blinds, and an air-conditioner groaned in the corner.

There was a TV, radio, books; in fact it seemed that virtually everything the family possessed was in this one room. Years ago when we lived in Rome, someone told me that at heart the Romans were in fact cave-dwellers. They always kept the shades drawn in their houses and lived in semi-darkness. Bruce seemed to be a bit of a cave-dweller himself. As the summer temperature was often well into the forties, I guessed he knew what he was doing.

The young man introduced himself as Glynn and asked us if we would like a beer. We gladly accepted his offer and he brought us a can each. Then Bruce loped in.

'Strewth, I thought I was bloody tall, mate. You only just got in the truck.'

He sat himself at the table where we were already positioned and cracked open a beer. I could tell he wasn't a heavy drinker. He was too lean, too alert.

'Jacqui'll be out in a minute.'

As though she was waiting for her cue, Jacqui entered and greeted us.

'You are very welcome,' she said with a warm smile. Her French origins were unmistakable. Even after years in the bush she had dressed for our visit with the flair and taste that is so natural to French women. Her face told the story of life in the bush. Clearly life had been hard but, like her husband's, her eyes sparkled with humour and vitality. She joined us for a drink and then prepared the table for a meal. As she brought out cold chicken, sausage, cheese and bread, she told us how she had come to Rabbit Flat.

'I was born near Paris. There I worked in a shop. I hated it. I had to wear stockings every day, no matter how hot the weather was. I had to wear stockings even when mushrooms grew between my toes.' I assumed she meant fungus, but didn't interrupt. 'My sister is still in France. My father is now dead but he came out here once. "Alice Springs I understand," he said. "But here?"'

She laughed with genuine amusement at the thought of her elderly Parisian father puzzling over the fact that his daughter was living in the middle of nowhere.

'I came to Australia in nineteen sixty-four and worked as a punchcard verifier with IBM. Then I met Bruce.'

Bruce could not resist an interjection. 'She's got bruise marks all over her arse where she's still kicking herself.'

They both laughed. Jacqui continued: 'It took me quite a time to get used to Australia. The bad language, for example. When I hear swear words in English I don't mind, but when they are translated into French I shudder. It's my upbringing, I suppose.'

More beer was produced by Glynn and we were encouraged to eat. Bruce declined.

'No,' he said. 'No. I'll eat later.'

I looked up at the wall by the table where there were several paintings. One was an unmistakable likeness of Bruce.

'Yes,' said Jacqui. 'That is my work. I like to paint from time to time.'

Bruce was silent. I could see that he was weighing me up. He knew that I had come to see him because I was writing a book, and he had agreed to see me because he knew of my experiences in Beirut.

As Jacqui poured coffee, Bruce looked thoughtful.

'If you'd been a bloody journalist you wouldn't have got through that bloody door,' he exclaimed. 'I can't stand the bastards. We've had them here in the past. "What's it like out here, Mr Farrands? Any trouble with the black fellas, Mr Farrands?" I tell them to bugger off, the bloody lot of them.'

I remembered that Bruce was known throughout the region as Bruce *Shotgun* Farrands, and smiled.

Bruce continued: 'It was Terry Underwood who thought that we ought to meet. The Underwoods are neighbours, but we haven't seen them for over twenty years.'

John and Terry Underwood were one hour's flying time away and we were due to stay with them later. They had arranged for me to meet Bruce and Jacqui, and already I was more than grateful for their introduction.

When we had finished our coffee, Bruce hitched himself up in his chair and rested his arms on the table. Like all good story-tellers he knew when the moment was right and the audience was ready.

'The two most common questions we get asked by the southern tourists are: "Do you get lonely living out here?" and "What do you do all day to stop being bored?" You sort of take that in various degrees. There's times you can't take it at all; other times you just shrug it off. I can try and see what they are saying from their eyes.

'Now, they have just come several hundred K to get here and all they've seen is bloody spinifex and a bit of sand with the occasional bush or tree. But, *Do you get lonely living out here?* Now, they've seen the physical side of it by driving endless bloody miles, but see, when we first started here in sixty-nine we lived under a mulga tree, under white-washed hessian and tarpaulins. The type of traveller that came to us in those days when the roads were up to shit and there was none of those flash roadhouses and motels and casinos (and I'm only talking twenty-five to twenty-six years ago), the people who travelled in the outback were very much like the people who lived in it. They had a bushy-type mentality and they didn't mind putting up with a few flies. If they got a little place and it only had tents they were so pleased that they could get a shower and they could get a meal and a drink of water. It was all appreciated. The years went by and the roads got better; the grits and gritter came in, and certainly in the eighties things went along at a mad pace until the crash of eighty-seven. October eighty-seven.

'So, the physical side nowadays, we're mainly talking about people who come out of these urban ghettos, who can't operate unless they've got a neighbour in each bloody pocket and one up their arse and one across the bloody street. I can't understand it, but millions go for it, so that's the way it is. But then to them just to get to the outer suburbs would be exploring. When they get to a country like this in a coach, the problem is compounded. The coach drivers are a product of that urban existence too. So we've gone from the intrepid traveller, if you like, of twenty-five years ago, and now get the ones that I call the Time Capsules, where they hop on to a forty-five-seater, air-conditioned, airbag-suspended, tinted-windows coach. You step into this Time Capsule from a suburban Melbourne and the crew are suburban, so you talk as you go along, no bastard is any the wiser. I don't know what motivated them to come bush in the first place. They see a show on TV or read a book or hear a story, then they spend two thousand dollars, hop into a Time Capsule and away they go. So, they talk Melbourne talk. By mid-morning they get out to have a convenience stop and that's the closest they get: the flies around their arse and their face. They complain about the bush and they hop back into the coach and away they go. Every now and then they will pull into a roadhouse where they will talk to other tourists. Very seldom do you get an intelligent question. That's rare. So, they talk to other tourists that come from another urban area somewhere else. By the time they get here from north, or south, they have been at least two weeks in the outback and broadly speaking ninety per cent don't know, they're not interested, not capable of understanding.'

Bruce paused for a moment. I suspected that this speech had been working within him for years. I had been told that he did not speak at length with visitors these days, but now that he was in his stride he spoke with a rough and endearing eloquence.

'I've got to blame the crews to a degree, but then the problem's compounded again. When the crews try to tell the people what it's really like, say to get on to black boys as an example, someone will report them for being racist, so they get hauled over the bloody coals by their company because it's embarrassing. So, we get people coming through here now that are none the bloody wiser three weeks later. They've spent two grand and they're none the wiser. Now, that's in your own country.'

He paused again. Jacqui, who must have heard many of these remarks time and time again, listened intently. Glynn sat quietly in the corner. His father pondered for a moment and resumed.

'"What do you do all day to stop being bored?" That's a question they always ask. Well, this used to be the bar inside here before we closed it. When this was the bar we had various signs up. We used to try and explain to people what we did.'

He indicated that he was referring to the room in which we were sitting.

'What I say to them now, *if* I talk to them, is, I say, "Look, the only way I can explain is, all the things you take for granted in suburbia, we have to create and maintain." I tell them, "You press the switch, or park a plug in a three-pin point, and you get power. You wouldn't think where it came from, but you complain about the bill in three months' time. You turn on and you get water." And then I get a bit cruder. "You go to the toilet, do your business and press the button. Do you ever wonder where it goes? Somebody empties your bloody rubbish. If the shit hits the fan in the street outside at two in the morning you lock the door of your three-bedroomed, air-conditioned home and you ring the police. The cops can come round and get their guts kicked in, but you don't get involved. You stay inside your bloody house." And so it goes on. Water, electricity, the rubbish, law and order, all things that are part and parcel of our very existence. They take it for granted. They don't see it. "Oh," they say, "aren't you lucky! You've got all this water and it's free." Water costs you thousands of dollars a bloody year to put down a bore and equip and maintain it. These people who come from their ghettos down south have got shit for brains. They really are ignorant about their own country. They have no intelligence.

'Then you see people come from Europe. When you can talk to them . . . Sometimes you can't. The Germans have got a bit of English; the Japs, you can seldom talk to a Japanese. The Swiss are pretty good. You get a more intelligent response from somebody from thousands of miles away whose brain is not clogged with preconceived ideas. That's all I can work it out to. You see, the Australians, because they come from continental Australia, they live down south and think they know all about Australia. They are actually very dumb people. They only know a little bit of their suburbs. The other thing they don't realize is that as remote as we are, physically, we would handle and talk with several thousand new faces each year. A lot you don't talk to. Most you don't. As the years have gone by, less and less.'

I asked Bruce if he provided accommodation for travellers. He explained why he had stopped.

'Nowadays we have an area where they can camp. I don't want to keep harping back to the black-boy situation, but you see it's a hell of a problem for people in outback Australia. You see, you are governed by your own personal standards and then by law to keep the place clean and orderly. Clean and orderly – OK? Now, when you come to the blacks and you've got alcohol and you've got isolation and you've got politics, it's bloody near impossible. The Human Rights and Equal Opportunities Commission insist that you don't segregate or discriminate. You see, we segregated for seventeen years only because we wanted to give the travelling white somewhere that was safe and clean and more orderly. So, we had the inside bar and the outside bar. As time went by that was against the law. We cut out the grog for black fellas back in nineteen seventy-four when four got killed just up the road from here on beer. We had to cut out the hard stuff very early. We were told that was racist and racially discriminating and so we started to serve again. Anyway, about six years ago there was a whole series of events, so we stopped serving hard grog to black fellas. For the next year we were still serving to the miners and tourists. Then we got the stripe again for discriminating. They said we were offering a different service, which is against the law. So, the vast majority of people down south don't know, and don't want to know, and people like us are stuck with it.'

I asked Bruce if he could tell me how he had come to the bush and what motivated him. He laughed out loud and Jacqui joined him. Glynn smiled gently.

'All right. I guess you're going to have to know that. I was on a station. I had thirty-eight days on my own and the manager and his wife were away. It rained and we were isolated. While the manager was away he met Jacqui and employed her as a home help. She had travelled around Australia and wanted a bit of station experience. They sent me a telegram asking what I wanted when they returned. I remember I said that I needed wheat for the chooks and some mousetraps. I also said, "Send along a long-haired mate." When they got back they said, "Here's your wheat and mousetraps, and here's your long-haired mate!"'

They laughed together affectionately.

'Anyway, we got married in Perth – I come from that way, see. We got married in February sixty-eight. We came back up to central Australia without a job. We had tucker for three months. We had three dollars, I remember, no job, and Jacqui's Christmas presents were a crowbar and a long-handled shovel. We had this idea, it was only a loose one, that we would go fencing for a couple of years, get a bit of a stake and then try and get a block in Queensland. They were breaking up some big places in Queensland. We were in Alice and we had both ended up working in town, when one day we ran into a station bloke who we knew very well from near here and he said, "Why not set up a tent motel at the Tanami?"

'Well, to cut a long story short, we brought a caravan out in May sixty-eight and set up the tents. It bloody rained all the time. We took twelve dollars in six weeks or something and that was from a Department of the Interior mapping team who were going through. While we were there a mining company came out and they brought all their stores and they gave us a job each. We were looking at aerial photographs one night. Of course, we wanted to do our own thing, but didn't really know what it was. We didn't want to go and work for wages and we knew we would never have enough money to own a station. I mean that's just unbeliev-able. But, when you're married, it wasn't a real proposition to go back to the station and live in men's quarters. Jacqui was a cook at the mine and I was off-siding on a little rig, and one night we looked at these photographs when this area was mapped by the army for the first time in nineteen fifty. The map you have is still from the original aerial pho-tography. We spotted this waterhole just to the back of the house on a nineteen-fifty photograph. So we came down to look for it. It was all Crown Land in those days. We pre-dated land rights. We found it. There was beautiful grass country at the back. Not enough for a station, but there would have been enough for a bullock paddock, so . . . We towed all our gear down here and put it under the tree next to the waterhole. This would be in mid sixty-eight. We went into town and spent the next eight months negotiating for a lease of land in Rabbit Flat in the middle of the Tanami Desert. No bugger knew where it was, of course. So then the government put all these covenants on us. You had to have improvement for so many thousand dollars for so many years. God knows what. We never had the money, so we had to look for backing. So, we went to Bill

Wilson, who had owned the four stations we had worked on, and with a verbal guarantee we went to public auction in early sixty-nine and we were the only applicants. We got a bit worried, as we thought someone else might have foreseen the future.

'We came out here in January sixty-nine. We lived under the mulga tree for about eight months and we graduated up here to part of a tin shed and just kept adding to it. The thing that hurt us more than anything, but you've got to learn to live with it, we had only been here about six months when the black fellas found us. We were thinking about tent accommodation for the tours. Then the blacks found us and the grog run started. They'd get here at three o'clock in the bloody morning! Fifty or sixty of them, yelling and bloody scrapping. In those days grog was just in a tent out at the front and we had no security. All I had was a point-twenty-two pump action rifle. I'd worked eight years on stations with station blacks and got on very well with them. Then I ran into settlement black fellas. See, they've been spoiled by handouts. Anyway, we've fought rearguard ever since. We fought land rights for five or six years. That was very traumatic. The worst years were seventy-six and seventy-seven when our kids were very young. See, the problem was that our land was up for grabs. It was all Crown Land and we had five acres. Then we got three added on, but it looked as though we were going to get kicked out when land rights came in. Of course, you're not getting support from the south, because they don't understand and don't want to know. That was a big hurt. No one was going to come here and support yer. So, we just had to handle it the best way we could. When you've gone through what you've gone through, and I'm not saying ours is anything as bad, but you do know what it's like to be tested over a period of time and if you come out the other end and you've got most of your faculties together you can look and say, "Well OK, what's happening now is not so bad."'

Bruce paused once more. The more he told his story, the more I could understand his anger against the south and southern-orientated politicians. His fight was a fight for life and for his own identity. According to Bruce, those from the south did not understand or even care.

'The thing I've tried to work out in my own mind on numerous occasions is why people would come out to this sort of country and put up with what we do. Now, speaking for myself, I think you have to be partly a social misfit. I say that in all honesty. If I was successful in getting on with people – I played sport when I was in third grade, but just say I was an extra good sportsman and I got on with people – I would not have wanted to get out of it. But of course, I was brought up in the bush and then had four years in Perth and that bloody near killed me. So I guess that was the motivation. I had to get out of the city. It was coming in on me. From there on I have trouble explaining it, because I went north in February sixty-one on the sheep stations and I just wanted to learn it so much. It was such a physical thing with me that I could bloody near eat it. It was a whole brand-new experience and I just loved it. I've been the same all the way, except on occasions when there were various problems, and there were times when you wanted to go but you knew that perhaps that wasn't a real option. As far as people are concerned, I think Jacqui can do without people more than I can. I like to have a yarn, but, I gotta be honest, I prefer to work alone unless it's someone I'm totally compatible with.'

'That's not me,' said Jacqui, as she burst out laughing. Glynn smiled shyly and continued to remain silent.

'If there's one bloke I can get on with real good, it's Glynn. We are getting on better and better as he gets more skills. We have our few little friction points from time to time, but he's really stuck by me the last couple of months. It's been real shit work, but he stuck by me.'

Bruce was clearly deeply fond of his family and they of him. Years of living in isolated conditions had forged them together and shaped their individual identities in a unique way. He knew that soon Glynn would be leaving home again and that neither of his sons would live in Rabbit Flat. As he went back to comment once again on the loneliness he had experienced in the past, I suspected that he was casting an eye to the future also. A future in Rabbit Flat without his sons.

'I've always been aware how lonely I was in the city. There were five hundred thousand people down in Perth when I was there. Over one million now. You could go years and not know your neighbour, and I can remember I lived on my own in a house in Little Italy for two and a half years. I tried desperately to get out to a little country town. I just had to get out of the city environment. As soon as I got into the bush it was as if the weights fell off. Even when I was on the stations I was never keen to go into town. You went into town and were pissed for a week, then no money, just a one-week millionaire. You always yearned to get back to the bush. It's a bit of a joke out here, but I have gone for up to six years without going into town. As I say to people, OK we've got the telephone. It's a digital repeating system that they have put in for people in the bush. Now, Jacqui's sister in Paris is only fifteen taps away on the dial. And it's as if you're in the next bloody room. So far as isolation goes, miles, yes, but as far as communication goes we had the radio telephone for thirteen years. It was a bit scratchy, but we were able to call friends on that. We've now got a fax – that's another step up. We're not into the computer stuff. Some people in the bush complain that we are second-rate citizens, but you have to remind yourself that we don't pay our way with the phone system. As much as I knock the southerners in the golden triangle, cross-subsidization gives us a phone system. We pay our way as far as calls go, but try and imagine what it cost to put that system in for a handful of people. If we had trouble here now I could get in touch with the police in Alice Springs and if they judged it serious enough they would come. They've done this in our radio telephone days.

'We haven't had trouble for years now to speak of. We've had occasions when we've had thirteen police. There was eleven came on an aircraft, two pilots, thirteen on the aircraft. It wasn't a police aircraft in those days. Also two paddy wagons came up. As for medical emergencies we've had three events at night time with hurricane lights and another couple by road. When the kids were born that was a whole story in itself and I think I should give you that one quickly.'

The story Bruce then told has gone down in the folklore of Rabbit Flat. The small map that I had been looking at before leaving Constantine contained brief items of information for prospective travellers. The bare outline of Bruce and Jacqui's story was printed on that. Bruce geared himself up for the final part of his saga.

'When Jacqui was pregnant, she had problems and she was told under no circumstances was she to drive anywhere. We've got what we call these Bangladesh butcher doctors, these Sri Lankans, and language is a problem. Also, they don't like talking to women, so it's a whole bloody cultural thing. Anyway, they suspected Jacqui was having twins and never had the sense to tell her, in case she panicked. Anyway, August the sixth, and the night of the fifth, nineteen seventy-five. We'd been very busy. We hadn't had a proper night, with only a station bloke here. We thought there was seven weeks to go. Jacqui got some meat out of the fridge to take some cuts of it and then she went to have a shower. As it turned out, the waters broke and we didn't really know what to do, because we thought that two weeks to the time we would send her into town. It would have left me on my own here, but there was no choice. So, she waited until the station bloke went and then she said, "You had better get the doctor. I think I might be starting labour." So, this is pre-digital radio, certainly. We had the Flying Doctor transceiver with the whistle. The double whistle, it was. You blew so many seconds into one, hit the send button and blew so many seconds into the other. If you were in a panic, the spit was running out of you and you garbled the message, or the hornets had built a bloody nest in it or whatever. It relied solely on pitch to set off an alarm at the other end for someone to come and do a verbal. Anyway, I am blowing away, blowing away, and there was nothing. Where I won it – and it took about two hours, I think – was every time I finished transmitting I identified myself saying, "This is Rabbit Flat from the Northern Territory. I've got a medical emergency." I said that if anyone could read the signal please get on to the Flying Doctor base at Alice Springs. That's what saved the day. There was a party going down the road that heard me, but they couldn't get me to hear them. Eventually a mission vessel in the Gulf of Carpentaria, for Pete's sake, picked up the signal on the skip. As you know, radio waves bounce off the ionosphere. They picked it up and got on to Isa. The Flying Doctor base at Isa rang Alice and told them of the emergency on 541a and could they get on frequency? So, Peter Robinson came on the frequency and I said, "Oh, thank God for that, Peter. Look, can you put me through to the doctor? It looks like Jacqui has gone into labour and I need to speak to somebody."

'So, they got Sister Ray Jones and it was agreed that the air-med aircraft would be out here at first light. It was governed by us not having night facilities, anyway – I was getting all that sorted out. Sister told me to keep her comfortable and said that she would see me in the morning. I'm just signing off. It's ten or eleven o'clock at night when Jacqui says, "You'd better get back to them. It looks as if this is imminent." So, I get back. "Peter, Peter, for heaven's sake get Sister Ray Jones." Well, Peter knew as much about childbirth as I did, and that wouldn't fill a bloody postage stamp, so he got Ray to talk to me direct. He held up the phone to the radio mike in Alice and she talked me through from Isa. I wrote it all down. Basic common sense, anyway. Jacqui really saved the day. We got the cotton wool out. It was bitterly cold, so we warmed it by the fire. The next thing, she goes into labour and pops Danny out. He's a twin. We didn't know at the time. I'm all fingers and thumbs. Where do you bloody start, you know? I'm just getting the bloody cord tied with butcher's twine when the next thing . . . Oops, here comes another one. This bastard was breech, feet first. We didn't know for months how lucky we'd been. I wanted to tug, but Jacqui had more common sense.'

As Bruce told his story, Glynn, the second twin to be born, sat quietly in the corner as he had done throughout. All through my visit he hardly spoke at all.

'Jacqui helped me tie the bloody cord and then, of course, the after-birth wouldn't come away. Someone said, "Didn't you panic?" Well, there's another thing: panic is a luxury, when you stop to think about it. It's easy to panic. If we'd panicked that would have been the end of it, so we just had to bloody knuckle down. So, Jacqui was sitting up helping me and about an hour later it came away. I tried to get back on the radio. It's one in the morning. Kids are always born at a mongrel hour. So, I'm trying to get back on, but of course I never could. I never made contact again. So, as we both hadn't been sleeping much, as we'd been very busy and were having trouble, I remember we both crashed, and the plane got here at eight in the morning. I walked over. I must've been in a daze. The sister was dragging white sheets out of the aircraft. She was all bust and bustle, you know? So she said, "How's Jacqui?" I must have answered in the plural. I said, "They're OK." And she said, "What do you mean, they're okay? Has she given birth?" "Well," I said, "yes. There's twins." "Oh," she said. "You're a darling," and she gave me a kiss. Anyway, she came over and they took Jacqui and the kids away, and they went into hospital under intensive care. It was touch and go, and they were under-weight to buggery.'

Bruce stopped and for a moment we all sat in silence. Although he had made light of the experience, I could imagine what they had been through. I looked across at the intelligent face of Glynn, the second twin, and then at Jacqui. Not only did I like this remarkable family, I respected them. Bruce and Jacqui had chosen to leave the herd and forge a life for themselves. Even now, twenty-five years on, life was hard, but by leaving the herd they had developed a strength of character that would be hard to match anywhere. They were survivors.

Neil looked across at me and held up his watch. 'If we are going to get to the Underwoods' by nightfall, we had better leave soon.'

He was right, but I didn't want to leave. I regretted that we couldn't stay for several days in Rabbit Flat. We stood. Bruce said that it would be good to get a photograph, and I produced a little cardboard throwaway camera from my pocket. I had bought it at the airport especially for this journey. We trooped outside. It was still hot. We stood in front of the roadhouse, and pictures were taken.

Bruce shook my hand.

'Remember,' he said. 'Loneliness is a state of mind. But I guess you know that already. You'll come back one day, won't you?'

I assured him that I would, and I meant it. One day I would return to Rabbit Flat along the Tanami Track.

We climbed back into the truck, and Glynn, as quiet and polite as ever, drove us down the dusty road to the plane. He stood watching us as we taxied to the end of the strip. I wondered if he wanted to be leaving with us. As we headed to the Underwoods', the next-door neighbours, we could see the three Farrandses looking skyward and waving.

I looked at the map and noticed the hills behind the waterhole. They were named the Farrands Hills. The land had left its mark on Bruce and, in turn, he had left his mark on the land. The solitary voice of Bruce and Jacqui Farrands would continue to sing across the years; would continue to echo down the corridors of memory. Their song was also my song.

Neither Neil nor I had much to say as we flew directly north to Riveren. As I examined the map I could see that the territory over which we flew was as sparse as our conversation. After leaving Rabbit Flat, we passed over the Black Hills, Wilson Creek and Hooker Creek. That was it. As there was no direct road linking Rabbit Flat with Riveren, and as the journey was over uninhabited territory, it was hardly surprising that there had been no neighbourly get-together between the Farrandses and the Underwoods for over twenty years. To the west of our route there was one homestead off the track leading from the Tanami Mine to Lajamanu. Then, a winding track ran from Lajamanu to the Riveren Station. Not an easy journey at the best of times and at the worst of times impossible.

As we flew in silence, I thought of Bruce and Jacqui. It was easy to see how anyone who had a superficial meeting with Bruce, and who took some of his comments at face value, might regard him as being racially prejudiced. But that was far from the truth. He had a respect for the old Aborigine. The one who was skilled with horses. The one who knew his trade and was in touch with his own traditions. That man Bruce respected. What he feared, and perhaps despised, was the alienated Aborigine. The one for whom native traditions had become nothing more than convenient bargaining tools. The one who could not, or would not, learn skills to equip himself for survival today. Perhaps Bruce had so little time for the alienated Aborigine because he knew instinctively that he himself could be that man. He too knew what it was to live precariously. He had wrestled with the spirit of the land and achieved an uneasy compromise. He was damned if he was going to be preyed on by those he regarded as having sold out to state handouts and cheap liquor. There was not a lot of room for sentiment, nor for political subtleties, in Bruce's mind. For him, as for all who inhabit the interior, survival was the issue. Survival . . . but not at the price of identity.

*

Before visiting the Northern Territory, I had never heard of Joseph Bonaparte Gulf. I mention it now because, between Turtlepoint and Quoin Island, both of which are at the end of Queen's Channel, the Victoria River empties into this gulf named after a former King of Naples. One of the delights of Australia is that it brings the most unlikely characters together in geographical conjunction. Riveren Station is placed some several hundred miles inland at the headwaters of the river. Terry Underwood once said to me, 'If anyone asks you where Riveren Station is, tell them it's at the head of the Victoria River.' I promised her that I would, and in anticipation of the question, I now have.

It had been raining when we landed at Riveren. Terry, all five foot two of her, met us at the airstrip. She too was dressed in outback kit, an essential of which is the Stetson, or its cheaper imitation. Once, on a visit to Texas, I examined these magnificent hats and was appalled at their cost. Nowhere was it possible to buy one without parting with dollar bills that ran into the hundreds. I decided that I really didn't need one, until Jack Allen, the former Presiding Bishop of the Episcopal Church, presented me with one in New York. He had been given several during his long career in the church and, as we shared head sizes, he decided that I might as well benefit from Episcopal generosity. I wore it once in Fifth Avenue when I went shopping with an American friend. We went into a large store and as soon as I opened my mouth it was obvious to the assistant that I was British.

'Who's he?' asked one counter clerk to my bare-headed companion.

He leaned across the counter and half whispered: 'He's a genuine Scottish oil millionaire.'

Not all outback hats are genuine Stetsons, but kicking around in the lumber room of many a remote station are empty boxes bearing the famous name and posted from Texas.

When Neil had secured the plane to the ground, we hopped into the truck.

'We'll drive over there,' said Terry, pointing towards the middle distance. 'They're bringing some cattle in tonight for shipping.'

We bumped off the track across the bush and Terry stopped the engine. A seemingly endless line of cattle stretched as far as the eye could see.

'How many are there?' I enquired.

'About two thousand,' she replied. 'We're a bit short-handed at the moment. We often have difficulties in getting staff to come and stay out here, so at the moment one of our sons and a cousin are helping out. We've just been rather badly let down. When we were in Sydney we interviewed two boys for a job on the station. We thought we had told them exactly what it was like: the heat, the hard work, the remoteness. They said that they wanted to come up and work, and they did. After one week one said that his mother was ill and he had to go home, and the other said he had to go with him. That was that. No matter how hard you try to tell people what life out here is like, they can never understand until they have experienced it for themselves.'

We watched the line of cattle moving towards us. Occasionally one or two of the more inquisitive would stop and peer at us over the fence. Then it began to rain. Terry started the engine and we drove towards the house.

Later that evening, when the cattle had been herded, John Underwood came in.

'John is one of the toughest men I have ever met,' said a friend of his to me when I was in Sydney. Now I could see what he meant. John was broadly built and well over six feet tall. His face betrayed years of living in the bush. His skin was weathered and his eyes revealed a reflective and good-natured individual.

He first met Terry, as a young man, when she nursed him back to health after he had suffered a fractured spine in a rugby accident. They married and she gave up nursing in Sydney for life in the bush. John seemed to have had more than his fair share of injury in life. He once went missing while piloting the farm plane. Next morning he was found hanging upside down in a tree, where he had been languishing for some twelve hours with several fractured bones. As if this wasn't enough, later he had the misfortune to be gored by a bull, and his body still bears the marks of that encounter. One needs to keep in mind that when accidents happen on a station, reliable help is often hundreds of miles away. Clearly it was an inspired choice when he married a former nursing sister.

That evening over supper, we chatted about life on the station. John told me how his mum and dad had come to Riveren in the 1950s with their three kids. Previous to that he had lived in the town, so he had been to school. When he got to the bush, his parents attempted to teach him by correspondence until he was twelve, when they decided he was impossible to teach, so they sent him to boarding school. He worked for a diploma at Gatton College (a farming college), then came back to the station, where he had been ever since.

For the first years he lived entirely with Aborigines out and about on the station. They came back to base every three months or so to collect rations and then were off again. Like Bruce Farrands, he had great respect for the old Aboriginal workers. He respected their skills with animals and their ability to survive in the bush.

He reflected on the Aborigine of today: 'There are many others who think that society is not helping them by pouring too much money into the situation. I hardly dare say that, because if I do I'm considered a redneck. Everything now is just money. They have to be able to solve their own problems. First, they have to send their kids to school, every day of the year, not just when they feel like it. Second, they have to stop kidding themselves about their own culture. When most of those kids grow up they are more interested in Western-type conveniences than their own tales. The young people are changing and the older ones are not recognizing it. We hardly employ any now, because they don't have the necessary skills and are not prepared to learn. The decisions about the Aborigines are taken in Canberra, and they don't understand the problem. The politicians try to appease the southern voters and if we say anything, then right away we are classed as redneck racists.'

Without any prompting from me, John Underwood had expressed exactly the same views as Bruce Farrands. I was to find this attitude right through the Northern Territory. The people who expressed it were not out of sympathy with the problems facing the Aboriginal people, but to a man they felt that serious mistakes have been made by government in dealing with the problem. It was not my purpose, on this journey, to explore these relationships, nor necessarily to present a balanced view. I noted what was said to me, however, as the issue clearly presented a worrying problem to those who lived and worked in the bush.

The following day, Terry sat with me in the large, comfortable living room and spoke about her experience of solitude. She was a naturally reflective person with many talents. She had written articles and was currently engaged in writing a book about her life on the station. She was also a skilful photographer, and several of her landscapes were dotted around the house.

'You've probably noticed that there is a lot of blue on this property,' she said as she poured me a cup of coffee. 'Blue doors, blue water tank and so on. That's to indicate we are on the headwaters of the Victoria River. I love it here, just love it.'

She told me that she had recently received one of my previous books and had started to read it. From it she knew that I had worked for the Anglican Church and she was interested in that aspect of my life. She herself was a Roman Catholic. She spoke slowly, and measured her words carefully.

'I grew up with faith. There was a disciplined way of life. Every Sunday I attended Mass and then . . . the plug was pulled when I came up here. In addition to religious security, other things disappeared. I knew that they would, but it was still a bit of a shock. There was no baby clinic, for example. I'm a professional and I prepared myself as best I could, but I went overboard. I became so good at being self-sufficient that I shut out the world. I didn't welcome people and I didn't meet people, because I was here in this wonderful place. I didn't miss the Sunday place of worship, because I was surrounded by creation. I mean that quite sincerely. There is such beauty in this country. I didn't realize that when I fell in love with John I would fall in love with the country as well. The cattleman and the country became two in one quite quickly. That gave me a shock. I felt very good here. Even more than happy; in fact I became quite emotional about the solitude. I just loved it. It absolutely soaked into me and I could be here for ever and ever on my own with him, which isn't on my own really. It is, in a way, because he was away at stock camps for one or two weeks at a time. I never felt worried, always secure. I felt less secure in the city where I was surrounded by people all the time. This was a place of peace.

'Then . . .' She paused. 'Then I was put to the test quite early in our marriage. There was a tragedy. Our firstborn son, Daniel, died when he was nine months old. How could we come back here? We left as three and came back as two. I found solitude the most hopeful and powerful means of coping. I think if I had been in an environment where there were people pulling, talking and pushing, trying to help, it would have been disastrous. The fact that I could come back here and work my way through it and not be distracted and not be interrupted and simply let this powerful country absorb me and me absorb it, that is how I was able to work through it. Solitude has been the greatest gift I have been given. As a nurse I worked very hard in a fantastic medical centre. I worked hard, played hard. It was a great life for a few years, but I saw an end to it. I needed some space and I found the biggest space in the world here. Even now I walk five kilometres every morning. I have to be in touch always with the solitary aspect of my life. Of course I can go into town and participate in things, but I don't feel as though I can give much, as I have given all here. John and I really do live as one. We can get in the car and travel all day to Katherine [the nearest large town] and not speak. But we are so close. It doesn't matter that there is nothing to say. Of course we have our grouches, life wouldn't be real without them, but I think that I would be so bold as to say that if I had not lived here, and married John, I am not sure life would have worked out for me.

'There are some negatives and I identified them very early on when I came here as a visitor. I was determined to avoid them, but I didn't. You have to try and overcome them. Solitude can make people, particularly women, very small-minded. A molehill can become a mountain. You get focused on it and it can bother you terribly, because there is nothing else. There is no chance of going out to lunch with your friends and forgetting about it. I was here for thirteen years without a telephone. That was fine. I talked to my babies and then I talked to myself. That's all right. I didn't always talk aloud. It was more an inner forming of ideas and a working through things, like you did in captivity. But there was a negative side. In the beginning I would get hooked up on ridiculous things. The danger is that if you are good at being on your own, silly things can be taken out of context. You can never shut out the world completely. I know, however, many in the world would have trouble living in the extraordinary solitude that we live within.'

As though to emphasize her point about shutting out the world, at that very moment the telephone rang. Telephones have a very loud ring on bush stations so that they can be heard throughout the compound. She dealt with the call and returned. Earlier John had told me that he found the phone useful, but never felt comfortable with it. It was also expensive. Terry replied by saying that it was wonderful to be able to keep in touch with her children at university and, considering that they spent very little on themselves, it was not really such an expense. There can be few families anywhere in the world who are in agreement about telephone calls.

She resumed her seat and picked up the thread of her argument immediately.

'Solitude does not make me over-introspective. There is no *over*. It's a question of balance. So, for six months, nine months or three years as it used to be, I would be here without going into town. Nine years passed without going into Katherine. When I did go into town I found it irritating until I got through the stages of knowing how to integrate again.

Babies did that for me. Children taught me that I had to go back into the world, but I am the city girl turned bush who made her decision and is very comfortable with it. In the early years, John was living in a very remote way. He would be three months in the country with nineteen black fellows before he came back here for flour and sugar. When I first met him I noticed his contentment. I came up here and couldn't believe the contentment of this man. Working, working, working. A very simple life structure. I always thought the city was fine when I was younger, but I needed to go further out. I never envisaged going out this far.

'The interesting thing is how our children approach another generation. They do cope very well. At first they may have been a bit behind in the classroom, but they soon got over that. They had breakfast here in this room where we are sitting. School was in the room next door. They would get to the door after breakfast and I would say, "Start marching." On the first day they replied, "What's marching?" So I would get in there and teach them myself. We had the radio, of course, but that was only for half an hour each day. I used the radio as a yardstick, so they knew how they were doing compared with other children on the stations. I wanted them to be so good, because it wasn't their choice that they were here without a teacher. But it was what happened here that was important. Lessons were sent out through the post. Before coming here I had lived twenty-three years in the town and had been through all that basic socializing. They hadn't. Then came the day when they were twelve and they were told to get on a plane, put on a school uniform and join a classroom with a teacher. Now all these things were new. The kids had grown up here. They grew up with calves and mustering horses. That was what they knew. Then at twelve they went to a whole new world. There were just the four of them here with me over an eighteen-year period. They had never even seen a school tie when they left home. At first they fretted terribly for this place which was their rock. This place was what they knew. But they adjusted very well. I once saw a TV programme when they interviewed two of our children about school life. You know, that was the most precious thing for me, because they said things that they had never told me. I was very moved.'

Terry returned to the subject of faith. She told me that when the children were at home the priest would come out every few months and take the communion service around the kitchen table. Now that the children had gone, he no longer came out with any degree of regularity, but they did get to attend church from time to time. There was a nice story concerning the visit of the Pope to Australia. Rebecca, her daughter, was one of three bush children chosen to ask the Pope a question via the radio School of the Air as the Pope flew over northern Australia from Melbourne to Darwin. Questions had to be submitted well in advance and Rebecca's question, "What is the hardest thing about being Pope?", was accepted. The family had to travel nine hundred kilometres for a dress rehearsal which was to be filmed in case anything went wrong on the day itself.

'Would you believe it?' said Terry. 'When the great day arrived the Pope blew it. He forgot to say "Over" when he had finished his remarks, so there was total confusion. The film crews didn't know where they were and so everything had to be filmed again afterwards.'

John came indoors and the three of us chatted together for a while. We spoke about retirement. Terry said she never wanted to leave the place. John said that when he eventually did it would be as well to leave so that his son had a chance to develop his own ideas without his elders breathing down his neck. We looked at some family photographs. There was one picture taken some thirty years before of a caravan parked next to a tin shack.

'Did you live in the van?' I asked.

They laughed.

'Well,' said Terry, 'I told my mother that I did, but in fact we kept all our stores in the van and lived in the shed until we were able to build the house.'

As we chatted, Neil joined us. As he worked for the Stanbroke Pastoral Company, and as John Underwood was an independent rancher, Neil had not been to the station before, so he took the opportunity to look around. It was here that Neil and I were to part company. He was returning to Constantine and another small plane was coming to collect me to take me to the next port of call. Neil bought a sealed drum of fuel from John to make sure that he had enough for the return journey, but as the rain clouds were gathering, he had to postpone his departure for twenty-four hours. I would be sorry to see him go. He was a splendid travel companion and an excellent pilot, even if he did forget to drop the wheels once in a while!

That night in my bedroom I took out my short-wave radio, plugged in the extension aerial and attempted to tune into the World Service of the BBC. It was raining and almost too hot to sleep comfortably. Eventually I was able to find an audible frequency and got Ed Stewart playing popular tunes. I had met him some weeks earlier when we were both helping out with a charity event for the Cystic Fibrosis Trust. He told me that the World Service programme was one of the most satisfying broadcasts he had ever done, as he received letters from every corner of the world. When he signed off, the news was broadcast. Here in the outback everything did seem so very far away. There was deep snow in London. Motorways were closed and here in the bush we were sweltering in the humidity of a late rainy season.

I thought about my conversations of the last couple of days. To me, Terry Underwood appeared to be a naturally reflective person who had grown into solitude in the most creative way. It seemed to provide her with a springboard for her many creative activities and she was conscious that it was an integral part of her life. Both the Underwoods and the Farrandses had emphasized, in their very different ways, the necessity of facing solitude squarely and growing into it. I was too tired and too close to the conversations to have any major thoughts on the subject. I switched the radio off, turned over and within a moment was asleep.

Constantly in my travels throughout the Northern Territory, I was reminded of East Africa. The significant difference was the sparsity of population. Here, one could travel for miles and not meet another living soul. Victoria River Downs could have been a compound in East Africa. There was an airstrip with a thriving workshop where mechanics were busy servicing single-seater helicopters. These machines are used more and more these days for herding the cattle, whereas in the old days that sort of work was done on horseback. What reminded me of the Africa I knew thirty years ago was the well-tended grass and the bungalows dotted here and there. Victoria River Downs (or VRD, as it was known locally), was about one hour by air from Riveren and was home for a community of about seventy people. I had landed there in the morning in a single-engine Beechcraft and was waiting for Geoff Brown to come and collect me in the plane from a station by the name of Newcastle Waters. It was hot and humid, and I sat under the shade of a huge tree sipping a cool drink and thinking about nothing in particular.

Eventually there was a droning in the distance and a tiny single-engine plane came into view and landed. The pilot jumped out, strode across to where I was sitting and introduced himself as Geoff Brown. He wore the traditional bush kit: shorts and shirt, with the real or imitation Stetson. For the manager of a large station he was young. He could hardly have been thirty, if that. We loaded up the plane and stepped aboard. Geoff turned the key and the engine responded as if it had a sick headache and didn't want to be disturbed. We climbed out and after much poking around under the bonnet, Geoff went to collect a battery. He thought we might be able to jump start it. A mechanic came over with a truck and tried the jump-start procedure. No luck.

'I don't know,' said Geoff as he took his hat off and scratched his head. 'I can't think what's wrong.'

As the sun was beating down on us, and as I knew as much about engines as Bruce Farrands did about childbirth, Geoff suggested that I went and sat under the tree again and when the mechanic had finished his lunch he would come and have a look at the plane. We had something to eat and another cold drink. After lunch, the message came that the mechanic wasn't feeling well and had gone to lie down. This, I thought, was getting more and more like Africa every moment. Eventually the pilot who had brought me from Riveren to VRD appeared with a box of tools.

'I'm not a mechanic,' he said, 'but I guess we might be able to do something.'

I don't know what he did, and he admitted that he didn't either, but within a few moments the engine roared into life. Acting quickly, before it stopped, Geoff and I clambered aboard and within moments we were speeding down the runway. Like Neil before him, Geoff was a natural pilot. The little plane in which we were now flying was basic and certainly didn't have all the sophisticated equipment that the Beechcraft Baron had. Humbert River Station, where we were heading, was only a matter of twenty minutes away, right at the edge of a wild open space known as Gregory National Park. The station house had not been lived in for about fifteen years. It had been used by ranchers from time to time, but in the main it had been left empty under the general care of a former grader driver, Ronnie. The station had its own notoriety, as it had been developed by one Charlie Schultz, who in 1928 developed what was a tiny run-down station into a thriving business. The story of this frontier post has been written up in a book entitled *Beyond the Big Run*. The true stories recorded in that volume make the Wild West look tame by comparison.

As we flew onwards, the terrain changed from the flat scrubland, which is so common in the north, to a fascinating rocky territory. Geoff pointed out acres of substantial soil erosion. We flew across a gigantic crater that appeared to be a disused quarry. Geoff told me that it was a natural formation. Deeper into the bush we passed over an Aboriginal settlement. The metal roofs of the houses glittered and shone in the bright afternoon sun. The rains had started in this part of the country and many of the creeks over which we passed were beginning to run with water again. As we approached Humbert, we could see the river. The previous week it had been virtually dry, but now it was starting to flow again. Little did I know it at the time, but the Humbert River was to become a river I would never forget!

Geoff put the plane down on the strip. As he landed, he had the clever knack of holding the plane inches above the strip to avoid puddles of rainwater that had collected. At the very last moment he touched down to make a perfect landing. He was indeed a natural pilot.

Once again a truck rumbled out to meet us. Darryn, who greeted us, had only been at the station for a few days. He was lean, burned by the sun and, like all station men, very tough. He had worked on stations all his life, but some time ago had left to work for the government. Now, in an imaginative move, he had been employed as a soil conservation officer for the region covered by the station. We drove across the river, which was running at a depth of about three feet, and made our way to the station house. His wife Roylene, a small, quiet lady, welcomed us into the house and apologized for the mess. They were both engaged in getting the house back into shape after years of neglect. It was a fine building, built in the African colonial style with wide verandas protected by fine-mesh netting.

One of the main reasons for me coming to Humbert River was to meet Ronnie. For the past few years Ronnie had been in semi-retirement, acting as caretaker for the empty property. Prior to coming to Humbert he had worked out in the bush as a grader driver and in that job had been totally alone for weeks and months on end. Ronnie represented a unique type of station worker and the story of his life could be repeated, with minor variations, by more than one old-time bush worker. Roylene suggested that I ought to meet with him before nightfall, as he liked to talk and he also liked to have a few beers in the evening.

Geoff Brown took me through the compound, past the workshop and into a small barn-like structure under which was a caravan. A puppy scampered down the steps of the van, took one look at us and retreated.

'Hi, Ron. Are you there, Ronnie?' shouted Geoff. He had to raise his voice, as a temporary generator providing power for the compound was chugging away by the side of the barn.

The puppy appeared again, followed by an elderly man stripped to the waist and wearing a baseball cap.

'Hi, Brownie,' he said. 'Good to see yer, Brownie. Don't worry about him. That's my little puppy. Sit down, Brownie. I'll get another chair.'

He disappeared inside the van and emerged with a canvas chair. After Geoff had introduced me and exchanged a few items of local news, he stood.

'I'll leave you now. See you later.' Geoff was a man of few words.

'Right, Brownie. Good to see yer. Take no notice of the puppy, Brownie. He's a real pal to me. Come on, Misty.'

He gently picked up the puppy and placed it on his knee. Ronnie wa[s] drinking from a can of beer and he offered me one. He had been expecting me, as Ken Warriner from Newcastle Waters had asked him if he would like to meet with me. He had agreed and had told Ken that he had enough stories to write his own book. He soon started.

'Well, it's like this,' he said as he handed me a stubby. 'My great-grandfather was a German. My mother and father were born in Australia. That accounts for my name, Estreich.' He spelled it out for me, slowly and deliberately.

'I was born on a dairy farm. My mother got killed in an accident. Well, you see my father went to town and was coming home in a car and there was an accident. He had had a few beers and tried to race the car across the bridge and there was an accident. My mother died in a room at the hospital. I was only five years old. I've got three brothers and four sisters. One is dead and I lost one brother in the war. He came home, but he died. The other one died from a heart attack. One brother is living in Sydney and three of my sisters. I don't know where the eldest one is – she could be dead by now. I haven't seen her for years. I last went to see them in nineteen eighty-one. I spent five months down there and I got sick of Sydney. I hated Sydney. After my mother died they sent me and Les and Eileen, Mavis and Hugh, they sent us all away to an orphanage in Sydney. That is where we were reared. I was there from five until I was fourteen. I was all right, they educated me. We used to spend some time out boarded with people and then they would send us back to the orphanage again. Then we would go out to somebody else, but we had to work all the time. When I was fourteen and a half, my grand-uncle, he owned a dairy farm, he wanted me to go up there, so he got me out of the orphanage. I used to milk thirty-three cows by hand, morning and night. After that I used to go out and plough, up and down the paddock all day, ploughing. If I wasn't doing that I was out digging bloody cockspur. I done that and then I was seventeen and a half. I got two shillings a fortnight.

'Then I used to go and work on the banana plantation digging up bananas. They grow them straight up the mountain there. I used to dig them up with a three-pronged hayfork. I worked with men and I made sure that I got to the top first. I used to beat 'em every time. Then I went boxing. I had eleven fights, then I gave it up. Then a good friend of my auntie and uncle had a job staking in Queensland. I didn't even know how to ride a horse. As soon as I got there, there were thirteen black fellas in the camp, all of them pure-bred Aborigines. I didn't even know how saddle a horse. The first horse I got on I tried to jump over a bush. He reared up in the air and I fell off him backwards. I was the only white man among them. They were good. They educated me. They taught me cattle work and how to work stock. They were good men. In those days they never used to get the dole or anything. We got twelve bob a week and lived on corned beef and dampers. We cooked our own dampers with flour and water, and perhaps we would have some potatoes and onions. To corn the meat we would get a killer [an animal selected for slaughter], cut it up and smother it in salt so that it would make its own brine in the cask. Then you would have to soak it overnight before you could cook it next morning.

'In those days the Aborigines, they were men. Today there is too much white blood in them. I see these bastards speaking about politics and all that. They are only talking for their own mob. They don't talk to the pure-bred Aborigine. In those days the pure-bred Aborigines hated the yellow fellas [people of mixed blood]. But now the yellow fella has taken over the country. I don't care if they come back at me for this. It's dead true. I was reared with them. They taught me how to ride a horse, how to throw a bull – they taught me everything I know. Everything I learnt I learnt off a black fella. No white man ever taught me anything. They were good men. I don't know. The country has gone to pieces. I can't understand what's happening. Look at these bloody politicians who are sticking up for the black fellas. They don't give a continental for the pure-bred Aborigines. All they are worried about is feathering their own nests. There are some really good blokes, pure-bred Aborigines, here. Old Riley and Snowy and Riley's sister Jackie. They are pure-bred Aborigines. One was born up by the creek and his sister under the big gum tree just over the other side of the house. I was head stockman for three and a half years, and then they phased the Aborigines out and brought in young white fellas. Then I pulled out when a horse rolled over on me and I broke a leg.'

Ron paused. He spoke with genuine feeling. When he spoke of painful times in his life his eyes would water. Although he presented a tough image, and was indeed a very tough man, he was also a man with deep feelings.

'Come on, Misty.' He put the puppy down and wandered into the van to collect more beer. 'This is a good van,' he said proudly. 'I was going to buy it when I retired, but Ken Warriner said he would buy it for me. He's a good man. And Bill Wilson. They are both good men.'

42

He returned to his seat outside the van and handed me another beer.

As Ronnie spoke of his life, in particular his early life, I thought that many people with similar backgrounds would have found a home in the army. I asked him if he had ever thought of joining up.

'Yes. I applied to the army when I was young. I had three brothers. Two were in Tobruk and one was in New Guinea, and I sent this letter away to the army. My auntie read it before I sent it and she also wrote to the army. She said that already there were three brothers serving in the army overseas and they'd only got this one left. So, that was it. One time I did contract mustering. I would break in three horses and keep one. For mustering I charged ten bob a head for bulls, seven bob for cows and three bob for calves. All I had was a tent. I have had a house, but I hate the towns. I like living in the bush. I was married. I married the station owner's daughter, but I couldn't get along with the mother-in-law. When I got a job as a head stockman, my mother-in-law wouldn't let my wife come out with me. She was only seventeen when I married her, see. I come home one weekend and had a blue [fight] with the mother-in-law, and I said, "If I wanted to sleep with you, I would've married you, for pity's sake. I married your daughter, not you."

'"Oh," she said. "Oh, this is my home."

'"OK," I said. "I'll move out."

'I've been on my own ever since. I've had four children, but only two with her. Only one loves me. The rest of them don't care, because they think I walked out on their mother. My wife married again and is still living, but I don't worry about it. She thinks I'm dead, but I'm not, you know. I'm still alive and I'll outlive them all. I've set my heart on that. My stray daughter loves me. I called her my adopted daughter and she calls me her godfather. I love her. Her mother was a German woman. I met her years ago when she was over here on holiday.'

Ronnie spoke at length about his adopted daughter. She lived in South Australia and he had been to visit her, but couldn't settle in the town. She frequently wrote to him asking him to go and live in the south, but he wouldn't go. He told me that when he died he wanted to leave what he had saved to her, and as he had not made a will, I urged him to do so.

'I'll do that next time I go into town,' he said. 'I don't want to live with a family. I want to be on my own. She says to me, "I'm a nurse. I can look after you." I love her but I hate big towns. One day it's freezing and the next it's bloody hot, and I just can't stand the change of climate. She says she won't come here because she doesn't like the hot weather, but I love my daughter, I really do.'

Ron's eyes watered again as he spoke. He stopped speaking for a moment and played with his puppy. 'Come on, Misty yer little bastard. She's a lovely little dog. So long as I've got my puppy I'm happy. I got her from some young black fellas. They were swinging her around and going to throw her away in the bush. I said, "What you got there?" He said, "Puppy. He no good. Mummy die. I'm going to throw him away." I said, "Give me a look at her." So I took it off him and fed her with a straw. Poor little thing couldn't even stand up. Only ten days old. Then I fed her with a spoon and then got one of those squeezer things which you keep honey in, and I used to feed her six times a day. Now look at her. Come here, Misty. Come here, sweetheart. I love animals, me. When I was a kid I used to go shooting birds. Now I wouldn't see anybody hit a bird. I've got loads of wallabies come up here. The black fellas chase them and they all come up here, cos they know I won't shoot them. I shoot dingoes, because they pull down poor little calves. I shoot 'em because they are a pest. I've never been able to shoot a brumbie [wild horse] in my life. We used to run them in the yard and break them in. If they have a broken leg then that's all right. We would shoot them to put them out of their misery. You see some silly bastards go out and the first thing they want to do is blow out a brumbie. I wouldn't do that. The poor buggers have a right to live, same as everyone else.'

Ronnie turned his mind back to living alone. 'I've been by myself since nineteen seventy-eight. All by myself. I like living alone, but I'm no loner. So long as I've got my dog I'm happy. I like to read, Wilbur Smith mostly. I love stories of Africa. I always wished I could go to Africa. I would have liked to go to a place called Zimbabwe, as I reckon that would have been good. I love animals, me, and I would have been right there. When I was grading, I lived in my van out in the bush. I'd get up at half past five and have a cup of coffee and a piece of toast. Then I would leave at about half past six. I'd cut a couple of sandwiches and take them with me and a bit of meat for my dog. I'd get home at five and fill up my grader and check her over ready for next morning. Then I would go in and have half a dozen beers, put my radio on and go to sleep. I didn't see anybody for weeks. The stores would be dropped off every fortnight. A couple of tourists might come through wanting to know where to go and all that crap. I don't worry about nobody. I like being by myself with my little pup. The happiest time of my life was when I first got married.

That was good, the first three years. My father-in-law and brother-in-law, we used to put bloody fences over the top of bloody mountains with a crowbar and shovel. When I was grading I used to go out shooting kangaroos on a Sunday. I've eaten emu, but it's tough as hell. One day I came home and there was no meat in the camp, so I see this emu. I only had a little point-twenty-two. I lay down in the grass and shot him. I cut a big slab off his rump and cooked it for about three hours. I had teeth in those days.'

Ronnie laughed and swigged his beer. 'Brownie told me that you were jailed for seven years. He said that you spent a long time in solitary confinement. They are unreal, these other countries. Sydney has hundreds of these Vietcongs. We went over there to try and wipe them out and what happens? They bring 'em over to Australia.'

I asked him about his religion.

'I'm Church of England,' he said. 'I was christened Church of England and married in the Methodist Church. Today the Church of England is about the same as the Catholic Church. I don't really care and I don't worry about politics or religion. If people ask me, I say I know more about cattle ticks than I do about politics! I'm a Christian and I lead a Christian life. I don't care what you are so long as you are a gentleman and lead a clean life. In the orphanage we went to church every Sunday morning. Sunday school, it was. I lived with a woman once. She was lovely, and married. I wondered if it was right interfering with her married life, but her husband used to beat her up and she was lonely, looking for company. He was a big strong bastard. I would have married her, but she said no, she was married to him and wouldn't leave him, and so I came back to the Territory and that was that. I love this place here. The only time I get lonely is when I want to be. Then I go into town and pick it up and as soon as I've had it I come home.

'Two years ago I had eight cans of beer and I had to go into Timber Creek. The copper there, I'd already given him a big parcel of grapefruit off that tree over there and then I had a couple of beers with Mark, a mate of mine. Next minute this copper pulls up behind me. I say, "Gooday, John." He says, "Ron, you've been drinking." I say, "I had a couple of lights down at the K." He says, "Come down to the station." So I went and he said, "Ron, we're going to book you. You read a hundred and nineteen. The reason we stopped you was because you didn't put on your blinkers when you were coming out of that turn." I said, "I didn't think you needed blinkers in Timber Creek."

'Anyway, I went to court and it cost me two hundred and fifty dollars. I said, "Tell that bloody judge I'll give him a thousand bucks to drop the whole case. Tell him I'll go down to the bank and get the money." The copper said he couldn't do that. The judge said, "I'll give you two years good behaviour and don't come before me for two years, otherwise I'll give you three months and a thousand dollar fine." It's all over now. He wouldn't accept the thousand dollars from me. Afterwards, I said to the copper, "*No more bloody grapefruit from my tree.*" They never took my licence. If I went to jail I'd go mad and kill the bloody judge when I came out.'

Ronnie stopped and looked up at the sky. 'See those clouds building up over there? We're going to get a big storm tonight, but we'll be all right, won't we, Misty?'

We had been talking all afternoon and it was time to stop. That evening Ronnie came to the house and had dinner with Darryn, Roylene, Brownie and myself. As he predicted, it was raining heavily and the rain continued throughout the night. The next day the Humbert River was some eight feet deep and quite impossible to cross with the truck. There was nothing to do but wait a while.

Throughout the next day and night it continued to rain. Not gentle rain, but the sort of rain that bounces off the parched ground with a primitive violence somehow appropriate to that wild and beautiful land.

The next day we walked down to the river, which had risen even higher.

'There is no chance of getting the truck over that,' said Darryn. 'I was once trapped for thirty-eight days,' he continued. 'Finally I was reduced to eating canned beetroot.'

We returned to the house, which seemed to be totally surrounded by cockatoos and frogs, both in full joyful chorus. Mosquitoes were beginning to gather as a result of the wet weather. Unlike Africa, there was no malaria and that was a small comfort. Over coffee, while Darryn was sorting out the outside workshop and Brownie had his head in some paperwork, I chatted with Roylene. She spoke about some of the old men who had spent a lifetime in the bush.

'Some of the old fellas who have been out in the bush a long time are victims of circumstances. Some become alcoholics. Whenever I've come across them over the years I've always thought that there is a story behind these old men. They've always been decent old men, even though they have been alcoholics. They have lived in the bush and worked hard.

They hardly ever developed what we might call social skills. They would go into town once in a while and get their pay cheque and, because they didn't have the social skills to help them meet a lady, they would go to the pub, drink their cheque, get thrown into the back of a paddy wagon and told to go back to the bush. That was their life and before they knew it they were old men. Their background was often a broken home or a marriage break-up. I remember one old man who used to have a sheep station in South Australia. Things went wrong and he ended up here in the Territory. He was a real old gentleman, even though he was a very bad alcoholic. He had ulcers and was always sick. But he did his best to look after the young boys on the station. He was like a father figure to those young helpers on the ranch.'

Roylene might have been speaking about Ronnie. Although she had known him for a long time, he had never told her his story. As it was, it was fairly typical. She clearly was a woman with compassionate understanding and it seemed to me that Ronnie was fortunate that, once again after many years, the station would be lived in and there would be someone around to bring him a little company in his latter years.

Like Sue in Constantine, Roylene had been a governess who had met and married a station man.

'When I first came to Humbert River, I felt as if I was coming home even though I had never been here before. The bush, there is something about it. I don't know, Terry, but I prefer to be here than anywhere else. Although our children are now away at university, and I miss them, I am happy to be here with just my husband. In isolation the family unit is strong. We have time to do more together, even as far as education goes. It's an experience for the parents and the children. We share everything and I never have any problems about getting away from the others. When we do get together with other people I have always enjoyed that time. We would go to VRD for a social outing or go to the Timber Creek races in September, and that was enough. I have never once thought that I was missing out on the company of other people or the fun and games of town life or whatever. People in the cities can be isolated. Sometimes more isolated than we are out here.'

Roylene told me of her work with the Isolated Children's Parents' Association – a lobby group that seeks better educational opportunities for geographically isolated children.

'People working on the land had real difficulty in making ends meet and thus had difficulty in getting their children secondary education.

They would educate them at home for primary education, but there were very high expenses involved in sending them away after that. A small delegation of bushy people took their case to Canberra and ICPA started the first branch. I have responsibility for the newsletter.'

We continued to chat about bush life as the rains continued to fall. I heard how Roylene's daughter Clare was bitten by a redback spider when she was just six months old. How she was airlifted out by the Flying Doctor Service and her life was saved. When she was older she fell off a horse and was evacuated once again. Such is bush life.

As we were talking, Brownie came in.

'We're going to have to get away somehow,' he said. 'We should make it now while the rain has stopped. If we leave it much later we will be trapped by the clouds again.'

I hadn't noticed that while we were talking, there was a break in the clouds and the sun had appeared for a moment. The phone rang. It was the mail service ringing to say that the plane wouldn't be able to get in today because of the weather, but would try on Saturday.

We went outside, where Darryn had found a small boat.

'The engine won't start,' he said. 'It needs some work, but this should get you over.'

Steam was rising from the wet soil as we packed our luggage on to the back of the truck. I said farewell to Ronnie and reminded him once again to make his will.

'I will, mate. Next time I'm in town. Good on yer, Terry.'

We shook hands and set off for the river bank, leaving Ronnie sitting by his van with Misty. Within a few moments we were at the Humbert River, which was in full flood. I took off my shoes and rolled up my trousers to the knees. Both Darryn and Brownie were wearing shorts. Darryn took a rope from the back of the van and tied one end to the boat and the other around his wrist. Brownie and I held on to the boat while he waded in until the water was up to his chest, then he started to swim hard. At first the current carried him downstream and he came to grief on a small island in mid-stream. We hauled him back and decided to push the boat upriver to a narrower crossing. I found it agony to walk across the sharp stones beneath the water, but the two station men appeared not to feel a thing. We found a narrower crossing and Darryn set off once more. This time he made the far bank and quickly tied the rope to a tree. Then Brownie, who was not a strong swimmer, set off holding on to the rope for dear life. When he was safely across, I clambered into the boat with the luggage and as quickly as they could they hauled the boat across.

We marched up the bank towards the plane like explorers of old, wet through and covered with red mud. As we had had some trouble with the plane before, there was concern as to whether it would start or not. If not then we had a major problem. We packed the luggage into the small hold, Brownie got behind the controls and, to our delight, the engine immediately sprang into life. My last sight of Darryn was as he retraced his steps to the river bank to swim back home. It had been a memorable visit to Humbert River Station. A most memorable visit.

*

It was early morning and dawn was about to break. Brownie and I sat together in the pickup by the side of the Stewart Highway. We had flown together from Humbert River to Newcastle Waters, where I had spent a few days as the guest of Ken Warriner, the man of whom Ronnie had spoken so well. Although by any standards Newcastle Waters was a remote station, after Rabbit Flat and Humbert, it seemed to be in the middle of civilization. It was a mile or so from the paved highway and about twenty-five minutes from the small town of Elliott. I had met Brownie's wife Anna, and young baby, and she had taken me to see the old settlement, now something of a tourist attraction. There was a small tin church, which was used once a year at Christmas, and the old Post Office and police station, now both disused. All were in the care of the National Trust. The house in which Ken lived was quite magnificent, having been built by Kerry Packer some years before. It was quite unlike any station house I had ever been in. It even had its own swimming pool.

Ronnie was right. Ken was a good host and a man with a long and valuable history of ranching, and it would be difficult to find a more experienced and capable manager. He told me that he was keen to see young people like Brownie take responsibility and develop new ideas.

'They will make some mistakes, but that's how we all learn,' he said as we walked around the station. 'It's quiet here now, but the boys will be coming in a couple of weeks and then we will be really busy. Brownie's a good man. He will do a good job.'

As I spoke with Ken, I thought about the Underwoods and Roylene and Darryn Hill. They shared common characteristics. All were very tough, reflective and careful with their judgements. It seemed that they had entered into a partnership with solitude; a partnership that had proved to be wholesome and satisfying. The same could be said of the family at Constantine. At Rabbit Flat, Bruce and Jacqui had certainly embraced solitude, but in running a roadhouse they depended upon other people so much more than the station families did. Their life had been one hard battle to achieve independence from the herd and for themselves. Solitude had formed them in a unique way, but life continued to be hard. And as for Ronnie, well, probably Roylene had said all that needed to be said.

We saw headlights flashing in the distance.

'Here it is,' said Brownie. The coach for Darwin was just in sight. We climbed out of the cab and collected the luggage from the back of the pickup.

'Come back one day,' said Brownie.

I assured him that I would. The coach pulled up and the driver climbed down nimbly to stow the luggage. I shook Brownie's hand.

'Goodbye, Geoff. Thanks for everything.'

He smiled, hitched his hat back on his head and walked to the truck. I climbed aboard, the door closed and I settled into my seat. There were TV screens along the coach and I hoped, against hope, that they wouldn't show films on this journey. They did. I closed my eyes and remembered Bruce's remarks about time capsules and air-conditioned coaches.

Darwin was eight hundred kilometres away and we would be there in the evening. I was sorry to be leaving the Northern Territory.

I must admit that this next visit was not planned; it simply happened.

After joining the coach at Newcastle Waters, I eventually arrived in Darwin, where I was met by my hosts for the night. We went for dinner at an open-air restaurant overlooking the ocean, but we didn't linger, partly because when coffee was served the heavens opened and we had to make a dash for cover, and partly because I had to be up at 3 a.m. to catch an early flight.

Back in London there was a message asking me to call my lecture agent in New York. I returned his call.

'It's about the lecture tour next month. We have a spare day and I wondered where you would like to spend it. You could go to the West Coast or even Salt Lake City if you wish.'

Some years earlier I had been on a flight that had touched down at this centre of the Mormon religion and I remembered the spectacular mountain scenery surrounding the city. I was also curious to see where those young men with dark suits and handy little briefcases, who had so often knocked on our door in London, came from. I said that it would be interesting to spend the day there.

'Right,' he said, as brisk as ever. 'I'll arrange it.'

Two days later, my itinerary and tickets arrived by courier and the following week I was on a plane from Atlanta to Salt Lake City. It had been a busy day in Atlanta. In the morning I had conducted a seminar for two hundred students, in the afternoon I had addressed some of the staff at the Carter Center and in the evening I had delivered a public lecture. I was glad to sit down for a breather. As soon as we were airborne the stewardess came up to me.

'I'm sorry you didn't recognize me,' she said.

Of course, as soon as she spoke, I recognized her. She had been on one of the first flights I had taken in the USA following my release and had protected me from the many well-wishers on the plane. As we chatted I could see that my companion, who had had his eyes closed when I joined the flight, was taking an increasing interest in our conversation. When we had caught up on the news of the last four years, and the stewardess had gone to serve some drinks, he turned to me.

'Say,' he said curiously. 'How come that dame remembers you after four years?'

His New York accent was unmistakable. I told him the story.

'Gee. Sure, I read all about that. Good to meet you.'

Throughout the flight we chatted. Jim was thirty, a manager in a high-tech company and unmarried. He had been born and brought up in New York and he described his move to Salt Lake City as like moving to another planet.

'It's very hard to meet girls there,' he reflected wistfully. 'Many get married at fifteen. Sure, they're divorced at twenty-five, but hell . . .'

As he described Salt Lake, it didn't seem to be too different from his own city. He claimed that it had the highest divorce rate in the country, one of the highest rates of drug and alcohol abuse, and suicide had gone off the top of the scale.

'I don't care what people do,' he said. 'It's their choice. But everything in Salt Lake is under cover. You can only buy liquor at state liquor shops. If you want a drink in a bar they will only serve you one ounce at a time. You can ask for a sidecar, but you can't have more than one ounce served to you in a single glass.'

I learned that a sidecar was another ounce of spirits served in a small glass, which the drinker was then allowed to pour into his one ounce to give him a New York measure.

'It's repression,' said Jim. 'Religion in Salt Lake represses everything. Some things are going to have to change in the future.'

*

That evening I was too tired to leave my hotel and after a light meal leafed through the tourist guidebook in my room. As I was casually turning the pages I came across the following entry:

Solitude – the name says it all. At one of Utah's famous Cotton-wood Canyon resorts with a base elevation of 8,000 feet, Solitude's beautiful glacier-formed, unspoiled setting offers 1,100 skiable acres of terrain with over 2,000 feet of vertical and 60 named trails. Take I-15 South to I-80 East toll, 215 South, Exit 6 and continue up Cottonwood Canyon.

'Vertical trails' confused me for a moment, but I decided that probably meant they were climbing routes. I had one free day only and during it I wanted to go to Temple Square and see the great Mormon temple. I had a picture in my mind of a colossal building set on a plane surrounded by snowy peaks. However, a visit to Solitude was very tempting indeed. How could I not visit such a place? I toyed with the idea of hiring a car but felt that might be catastrophic, if only because the directions were so confusing. Where and what was I-15 South? How far was I-80 East and how would I know when I had arrived at that particular exit? No, that was too difficult. With only a few spare hours my timing had to be exact.

The concierge at the front desk of my hotel solved my problem. There was a ski bus leaving for Solitude from outside the hotel at eight thirty in the morning, which would take me directly there. There was no return bus until late evening. If I only wanted to pay a brief visit, then it would be possible to work my way back to the hotel by taking several different buses once I had got out of the canyon. I needed no further instructions.

Next morning the weather was beautiful. On the edge of town the mountain peaks were covered with snow, the sky was blue and the air surprisingly balmy. As I waited for the bus, wearing a blazer and carrying my briefcase, I felt somewhat foolish. All my fellow passengers were togged up in colourful ski outfits and each carried at least one pair of skis. The bus trundled to a halt and skis were fastened to rails along the outside of the cage. As I climbed aboard, the thought crossed my mind that I could easily be mistaken for a Mormon missionary with my case and clothes! The bus was fitted with one of those awful machines that grab and swallow dollar bills and on no account will give change. I was a dollar short, otherwise I had a twenty dollar note.

'No problem,' said the surprisingly good-natured bus driver. 'Take a seat.'

I sat among the multicoloured passengers and stared through the tinted glass windows. The suburbs of Salt Lake City are like the suburbs of all American cities; hamburger joints, car showrooms, credit agencies and computer stores continued for mile after mile like some dreadful consuming disease. Then suddenly we reached the highway, the driver accelerated and we were off at full speed for Cottonwood Canyon.

The canyon was lovely. Soaring around us were mountain peaks. A small stream tumbled alongside the road and snow glittered in the bright sunlight. We climbed steadily, negotiated several very steep bends and then . . . there it was! A dark blue sign announced for all to see: *Solitude*.

I was the only one to leave the coach – the others were going to the terminus at Brighton, just a mile or so up the road. I stepped down and the bus drove away. It was midweek and the end of the season, so Solitude was almost deserted. A couple of empty ski lifts churned away, while a few novices trod gingerly over the snow. I walked across to the blue sign. I would have liked the sort of photograph that graces so many family albums, of the intrepid traveller standing beside his remote destination. Appropriately enough there was no one around to take a photo of me in Solitude, so I contented myself with taking a picture of the blue sign. Then I went back across the car park and bought a large floppy fishing hat from the ski shop. Emblazoned across the crown was the word 'Solitude'. *If this visit is included in the book,* I thought, *I'll wear this hat at the launch.*

I wandered some distance away from the slopes and sat still for a while. I hoped that Solitude might remain unspoiled, but I somehow doubted it. There were signs of some new building work nearby and the car park, although almost empty at that time of year, was vast. I pondered on the difference between the open spaces of Australia and those of the USA. In the USA, even in a remote location, one always has the feeling that the country has been 'tamed'. That around the next corner will be a Coca-Cola sign or a fast-food store. In the wilderness of Australia it continues to be possible to feel the great spirit of the earth, just as it is still possible to discern that spirit in Africa. In most parts of the USA the spirit has been either domesticated or banished. However, I was glad that I had made the effort to visit Solitude. Reluctantly I made my way back to the temporary bus stop, caught a bus to the entrance of the canyon and then took several local buses into town. As we travelled through the outer suburbs virtually every passenger who boarded was grossly overweight. Not just by a pound or so, but massively overweight. They heaved themselves on board and collapsed in a breathless heap on to the first available seat. I remembered the comment of a friend who once said that obesity in the USA was a sign of deprivation, not of affluence. There were also many elderly, sad-looking people. A bearded, worried-looking man on crutches sat opposite me. Someone recognized him and asked him where he was going.

'To collect my welfare check,' he said. 'They didn't send it this month.'

A heavily built blind man sitting opposite him joined in the conversation. 'I've got five dollars to see me through to the end of the month. That's all. Five dollars.'

No one answered him. Jim had said that one of the reasons the Mormon Church was among the fastest-growing churches in the States was because they would agree to help any converts with their outstanding debts on condition that, thereafter, they contributed ten per cent of their income to the church.

That afternoon I visited Temple Square, which was not at all as I had pictured it. The temple was so much smaller than I had imagined and, probably because it is always closed to the general public and unused by the faithful except for special occasions, it looked dead and lifeless. I went into the visitors' centre, but made a rapid exit when a couple of 'guides' headed in my direction. The domed church was open to the public and I went inside. Someone was playing the organ and I stayed to listen for a while. It would have been enjoyable to listen to the famous choir, but their rehearsal was not until the following day when I would be far away in Washington State.

I thought about Jim's remarks and wondered if they were simply the cynical remarks of a New Yorker or whether they were true. In my walk through the city, during the middle of the afternoon, I encountered one man crawling along the pavement. From a distance I thought he had suddenly had a heart attack, but as I drew nearer I could see that he was hopelessly drunk. He wasn't the only drunk I saw that afternoon, but then what does one see on the streets of most cities these days? On the way back to my hotel I passed the site of the former Salt Lake Theater, built by President Brigham Young and dedicated in 1862. 'The people must have amusement as well as religion,' said the former president of the Mormon community. His words were set in bronze on the wall where the theatre once stood. It had been demolished many years ago, and the building was now the headquarters of a telephone company.

I had been in the city for far too short a time to make any judgements about it, so I didn't. But I was glad I had made the effort to find Solitude. That was a pleasant surprise and that lovely little place in the mountains had not disappointed me.

7 Chicago

It was cold when I arrived in Chicago after one of those nightmare journeys when travellers vow never to fly again. There had been severe flooding somewhere in the south, and such is the interrelatedness of air travel that a problem in one part of the USA spreads throughout the network like a virus through a computer, causing chaos across the whole system.

'Hi, folks. This is the captain speaking. Chicago Air Traffic Control tells us that the place is seized solid. They have forty flights waiting to depart. They can't give us a slot yet, but we shouldn't be longer than two hours. We'll keep after them every twenty minutes or so. Sorry about this, folks.'

We waited longer than two hours and eventually arrived in Chicago's frantic airport terminal late at night. Everyone was talking about a recent air disaster in which a young girl of seven, attempting to fly across the country, had crashed on take-off, killing herself, her father and her instructor.

'It was a very American thing to do,' said a native of Chicago when we were talking about the incident. 'Only in America could that happen. Only in America.'

I was passing through Chicago on my lecture tour and had arranged to see a friend from Africa who was doing a postgraduate degree in the city. She was a Dutch medical doctor whom I had met some twenty years earlier in Ghana. She had gone out to Africa as a young medical volunteer and stayed on, eventually taking Ghanaian nationality. She had remained unmarried and had spent many years in isolated regions of Africa. I telephoned her from England, told her about the book I was writing and suggested that she might have some observations to make. I also asked if she could put me in touch with someone in the city who lived a solitary life. She was able to give an immediate response. While studying at the university she had found a room in a residential hotel where there were many long-term residents, and a number like herself who stayed for a year or two. One night she was disturbed by the sound of someone shouting and crying for help. She went out into the corridor and discovered her neighbour, an elderly man whom she had not previously met, in a state of some distress. She didn't go into any detail over the phone but merely said that she was able to help him and he seemed to be totally alone. I asked her if she thought he would like to speak with me. She said that she would ask him and later in the day phoned back to say that he would be glad to do so.

I travelled to the outer edge of Chicago on the elevated railroad, or L as it is known locally. If the poor travellers on the bus in Salt Lake had looked depressed, then the passengers on the L had them beaten. There was the usual contingent of the obviously mentally disturbed who ride the transport systems the world over. The expression of sheer misery on the faces of so many was tragic to see. What do the great cities of the world do to their poor inhabitants? We travelled through the depressing mess of dilapidated buildings that accompanies most inner-city railway tracks, while an African-American passenger stood and delivered an oration to an unresponsive audience. I couldn't understand a word he said.

I emerged from the railway station and walked the few hundred yards to the apartment block. It was situated directly on the edge of a high-crime district, although the block itself was elegant and well maintained. My doctor friend had one small comfortable room and a bathroom. The most attractive feature was the open view across the lake. She made some tea and we caught up with the news.

'Before we talk any further,' she said, 'I ought to give Sammy a ring to let him know you are here.'

I had telephoned him earlier in the day to confirm my visit, but had only been able to speak to his answering machine. She dialled his number and spoke for a moment. When she put the phone down she smiled.

'He seems a little confused. He thinks that you phoned to cancel the appointment, but he is happy to meet you.'

There was a knock at the door and my friend answered it. An elderly man came into the room. He was dressed in a singlet and trousers, with his braces hanging around his thighs. His hair was greying and ruffled. He wore a neatly clipped moustache which was quite grey. We exchanged greetings and he suggested that we go next door to talk. His apartment was exactly the same as the one we had just left. The central heating was going at full blast and although it was a cool day, the room was like a glasshouse. There was one armchair and a pile of newspapers was strewn around it on the floor. An unmade bed stood in the corner and there were two or three kitchen chairs scattered around. Although the room was untidy, it was clean. I imagined there were thousands of people in this city who lived just as he lived, and thousands whose conditions were far worse.

I began by explaining my reasons for wanting to talk with him. Without any further prompting he began.

'I lost my wife in nineteen eighty-two on the day they killed this black guy.' He struggled to remember the name and I suggested Martin Luther King; he probably meant the anniversary of king's death on 4 April 1968). 'That's it, yeah. Her death had a bad effect on me. I'm the type of person who has to have people. So it's hard, but you've got to keep fighting. You can't stop. I used to drive a cab and somebody, I don't know, he was about eighty or something, he said, "I'd like to be dead." I said, "Don't be silly, life is good." Now that I'm seventy-seven, I've lost a lot of friends and they've moved away to different places. Now it affects me. It bothers me. I fight it off. I'd rather be with people, so I'm always on the telephone and talking with people in order to shake this. I go to a lot of theatres – sometimes that shakes it. But it's tough.'

I asked him if he had children and he said that he didn't. He had been married twice and had relatives in Los Angeles whom he went to see on occasions. He returned to the subject of his loneliness.

'My mind floats back. You see something and it goes back to your wife. Recently I lost a friend of mine who was a friend for fifty years. He passed away. The doctor told him he should go to a psychiatrist. The fact is, that was the worst thing you could tell this guy. He had a home and some help but after a while the helper couldn't stand him. So his daughter couldn't get anyone to stay with him, so she took him in. After a while they put him in a rest home and he died there. He wanted me to get him a gun so he could kill himself. I told him, "Forget about it."'

We remained silent for a moment. I asked if the thought of suicide ever crossed his mind.

'I love myself too much to go and do something like that. But there are people who do it. Many a time it crosses my mind, but then I always come backwards. I'm not stupid. Of course, there are people in different circumstances of living. Their Social Security don't carry 'em. They would think about that. There's a lot of people being taken advantage of. Like people that steal their pension checks and everything. When I was working I would take people to the currency exchange and they would tell that to me. I said, "Why don't you go ahead and put your money in the bank, where your money is safe?"'

He paused again. I thought of the grim, worried-looking people on the train. Of the thousands of people who wandered through the streets of the cities of this world, isolated and despondent.

'I see people I know' cause I was in the cab trade, see. We meet from time to time, but I'm not seeing anyone who is close. My brother is in California. I telephone him once a week. But the worst thing about being alone, is being alone. That's it. I used to have friends, but they all started to go. The best man at my wedding, my first wedding. We went to school together. I had lived in his home. I was going to see him when he was in the hospital. In his case he ended up with cancer. All he would tell me was that he was worried about his wife. He doesn't have to worry about his wife now: he's gone. The same day that he went another friend passed away. You lose this one, you lose that one. I have a friend of mine who lived in the apartment next door. He went home to Illinois. I keep losing these people. Being alone is like being on the sea in a row boat with no oars. Then sometimes I feel sorry for myself. But like I said, I'm not going to kill myself.'

He emphasized this last remark as though he needed to convince *himself*, as well as me.

'I'm Jewish and I believe in God, but I don't believe in anything beyond death. I figure when you're dead, that's it. I don't like the idea of thinking of death. I don't have much to look forward to. I'm at an age . . . I don't look for women at my age. The younger ones only want money, so if you know that it keeps you away from things you ought not to be doing. They will make a sucker out of you, you learn. I don't sleep too good. I was taking some pills and they were not so good. I got sick. I was in here and I didn't know what was wrong and I blanked out. Your friend heard me crying out, "Won't somebody help me?" I was thinking that I would call my friends, and the funny part was I was thinking that I was in the trailer. I was calling my relatives in California and I thought I was there. I don't get too much sleep now, but when I do I get bad dreams. I sleep for about four hours then I wake up and my mind starts working. You are alone and you think of all those who have passed away. When I lost my baby brother, who was the last one, I said, "Why him?" He'd got everything to live for: the family, a job. I've got nothing. Having money don't solve it. It makes it easier, but it don't solve it. The situation could be different if I could find somebody that was grown up mentally. That would be the best thing in the world. Somebody to share with me. I just mentioned to my brother that I was going to leave what I have to his son. He can't help himself, he can't work or nothing. All of a sudden I got so much attention, it was so obvious, and my brother said, "Well, you should make a will out, write down what you've got." Then I started thinking. This is a very mean town. The people in this town don't even consider what you might be going through. They think that if you got money, well, you want to make a will out for me. I can't trust anyone in this place. No, none of 'em. You're in a big hotel and I don't know too many that are here. I try to go places where there is somebody that I know, like I go to California. I think that your book ought to have people looking to find out when their time is coming. If you put my name in your book, put my right name. It's Davies. Some people think it's Sammy Davies Junior, but it ain't.'

He gave me a wry smile. I asked him if there were any places that he went to in order to meet with other people.

'No. There are places for old people, but I don't go. You'll realize from the way I talk to yer that the mind ain't old. It's just the body. These people have these old ideas in their mind. It don't work with me.'

'Do you think solitude is something to be feared?' I asked.

He thought for a few moments.

'Well, when you say "fear", it's more or less that you're in the dark and you can't overcome it and you can't take it over. Things that are awful in your life come back to you. I was in jail for nine months. In a regular jail. I was fighting it all the time. When I was young I went with some people and I was the driver of the car which stuck up this truck driver. When I was in court, the attorney said something so when the judge got to me I put around that I didn't have anything to do and that I needed this and needed that. I wound up with nine months and the other guys got fifteen years apiece. Only recently it come to me, this business of death. It's so final that you don't have to worry about it. Nobody can help you.' He paused. 'I couldn't have taken what you took. Five years alone in jail. There is something else to life. If you don't have people I think that turns yer right around to wanting not to be here.'

There wasn't a great deal I could say. He didn't think he could take five years alone in jail, but he was already in jail. This overheated room with a pile of newspapers and the remnants of a half-eaten ready meal was his prison. Chicago was his prison. His body was his prison. The complex factors that weave together to form an individual life had bound him across the years and the only release he could imagine was death. We sat together a while longer.

'I will write to you when I get back home,' I said, wanting to extend some small human companionship towards him. He nodded and showed me to the door. I went next door with a feeling of sadness.

'You know, my friend, old age needn't be like that, need it?'

As I spoke the words, I knew that old age was like that for millions of people in the USA and beyond. I tried to think of old people I had known who were serene and at peace with themselves and had been able to convert loneliness into something more positive.

As I write this account, some years later, I remember my late mother-in-law, who died at the grand old age of a hundred and five. Living as she did amid the troubles of Northern Ireland, and also having suffered family tragedy, she was still able to live life to the full. Until the very end she read widely, was an accomplished watercolourist, and kept in close touch with her family and many friends. Although her physical body gradually failed, up to the age of one hundred and four she lived quite contentedly on her own, at peace with herself and the world in which she lived.

My friend poured two glasses of wine and we sat by the open window.

'No,' she said in reply to my question. 'But this is a hard country and a hard city. I don't want to give you the idea that my experience in America has been all negative. It hasn't. But I saw the dark side of freedom that night when I heard a voice crying in the room beside me – "Help me . . . help me . . . help me." I called the desk right away and all they could say was that it was nothing – just somebody in the street.'

From where we were sitting we could see the street several floors below.

'You know, we don't even have each other's telephone numbers here. It's so different from Africa. The old man continued to shout, so I called the desk again. They said that they would phone him, and a few minutes later I heard the phone ringing in his room. Then it stopped and nothing happened. So I called the desk again and they said that they had phoned but got no reply. I said that was probably because he was lying on the floor and couldn't pick up the phone. I went into the corridor and stopped by his door. I could hear a voice coming from down low, so I knew he was on the floor. Then I asked them to send someone up with the key so that we could help him. That took about half an hour. Then one of the workers, a Filipino or a Mexican, he came and he too heard the crying. He looked at me sort of shyly and told me to wait. He would be back. I thought that there was probably a law in this building that requires two people to open the door.'

As we spoke, the light was fading across the lake. A police car wailed in the street below. My friend stood and gently lowered the window. For a moment, I remembered her in Africa sitting behind a small table under a tree while a long line of patients waited to see her. She was young then. Now she was in her fifties, her hair was quite grey and her face bore the marks of long years spent in the African bush. She had aged physically, but inwardly she had retained, and deepened, the compassion that had first propelled her from the comfortable security of Holland to work among some of the poorest of this world. I could understand how the over-cautious society of the USA both puzzled and repelled her.

She sat down and resumed her story. 'Now I was getting desperate. I called Bob, a friend of mine who lives in this block. He has more authority in his voice and I asked him to speak to the front desk. The same person came back up again and Bob told him to open the door and we would take responsibility. He did it and then sort of ran away. I tried to enter, but I couldn't because the man was lying against the door on the floor, obviously confused. Once again I called the desk and they wouldn't come up, nor would they call the manager. Eventually a registered nurse who lives in the building came up. I had managed to get into the room and had lifted him on to the bed. I asked him if he would like the nurse to help him and he said that he would. I asked the nurse to come in, but she wouldn't. I found it all very strange and it was only later that I learned about all the legal implications. Eventually the police came and they told me that they could do nothing against his will. Sam wanted to stay in his room. I told him to leave his door unlocked and if he wanted anything to call me.

'Next morning I went to see him. He was still confused. He was speaking to his relatives in California and telling them he was at the station and would they come and pick him up. So I took the phone and told his sister that he was ill and they had better get hold of the doctor. Then I had to go to the university, but before I went I told the desk what I had done. They said it was none of my business and they would take care of it.

'Later I told the story to colleagues and they said that with all the laws in America everyone is defensive. They said I should not have gone into the room, nor should I have lifted him off the floor. If there had been a problem I would've been responsible. Well, while I think no country has it all, this country is really poor in the sense that it has over-idealized privacy. *Don't come into my space. Don't come into my freedom.* It's not good. It creates a defensive climate.'

My friend poured more wine into my glass. 'It's good, eh? You can get nice wine in America. I don't drink much myself, but it's nice to relax here in the evening and look out across the lake. I'm very lucky to have this room.'

We turned our thoughts back to Africa. The place that had made an indelible mark on both our lives.

'It was hard to come to America at first. I had a very tough time. It was such a transition from rural Ghana, where everyone was so friendly and so open. I don't want to idealize that, but there is an open door there and a community spirit. I remember coming to this town for the first time. The tall skyscrapers and the feeling of alienation. The sun couldn't even reach the streets. There was a greyness. A great overpowering greyness. People would say that Chicago was a wonderful city with a wonderful culture. Yes, I want to respect them, but I don't see any beauty in this concrete, six-million-mass storehouse of people.'

My friend had attempted to bring something of the past to her small room. There were several of her paintings and some photographs of the mentally disabled children she had cared for in Ghana.

'I begin to like this room,' she said. 'It is sort of compensating for the extremes of openness and public life in Ghana. I begin to like my little space here. I have come to value privacy, and when you talk about solitude I am trying to build up my own solitude. I need my homecoming to be in solitude in order to be in my inner peace. I need my own space where I can unwind, and that is very different from loneliness. Even in Africa I needed that space. When I think of solitude, I think of a fearless place where there are no demands. Where there is no pressure of business. Where I can come back to myself, come home to myself. On the other hand, solitude has almost made me sick with agony. Sometimes, when I was in Africa, there was the solitude you get when you are with people you only half understand. Everything is different: your culture, language, educational level, value system, everything. You are alone, and I have experienced that aloneness and have found it very tough. There were years when I was very down, cried a lot and was very depressed; wanting some friends, some real connection with others.'

She spoke with feeling – the feeling that I understood. I too remembered times in Africa when I felt sick with loneliness. Somehow Africa put me in touch with my primitive emotions and they scared me. Africa made me conscious of the rough brutality of nature, as well as the supreme beauty of the earth. It made me feel my vulnerability in life. I asked my friend how she coped with her loneliness.

'When I was a student, before I went to Africa, I lost religion. I didn't want God. Africa gave me spiritual values so that I found I really wanted God. That connection with God, even though it keeps changing and developing, is important. In times of desperate loneliness I would fall back on that connection. Also I would do writing. I love writing. I would paint. At one time in my life I did a whole series of paintings and that helped me process some of the agony of being disconnected. Other times I have laid on my bed and cried, but that doesn't work. When I look back on the hard times of solitude I think it was right, it never harmed me. It may have given me pain, but it helped me to grow and understand myself better. It was a positive experience coming out of a painful experience. I remember times in the desert in Africa when it was wonderful. There have been some wonderful experiences, and some terrible experiences when I thought that I wouldn't make it. There were times when I would over-work, which is what you do in the bush. You can burn yourself out in taking care of others. In the end I think that it has given me both ways, the shadow and the light side, and now that I look back I can see it in balance. But at this moment, I am in transition. Now it will soon be time for me to go back to Africa and I find it hard to say goodbye here, even though I want to go back.'

It was now dark. Across the lake the lights of a boat flickered in the distance.

I said, 'When I was speaking with Sammy, he told me he was haunted by memories of the past. Are you?'

My friend looked directly at me. 'No, not at all. You know that I've been through different stages in my life. I left the church and then reconnected. There were times when it faded away and I thought that I was losing my faith again. A few weeks ago I went on a silent retreat. It was truly silent. We sat for ten days without speaking at all. There must've been about forty of us and on the final day we were permitted to speak to each other. We didn't want to talk about where we came from and that sort of thing. We wanted to hold on to the peace that we had found. It didn't come easily, but when I went away I felt really creative and somehow whole. It was good.'

I stood. It was time to leave. We walked together along the corridor and down to the front lobby. The desk clerk nodded and smiled at us.

'Perhaps the next time we meet will be back in Africa,' said my friend. 'Who knows?' I replied. 'Goodbye, old friend. Thanks.'

I walked along the street towards the L. The lights from the ship on the lake had disappeared. In Sammy's apartment a steady light burned. I remembered the words of Walt Whitman from 'One Thought Ever at the Fore':

> That in the Divine Ship, the World, breasting Time
>   and Space,
> All Peoples of the globe together sail, sail the same
>   voyage,
> Are bound to the same destination.

It was mid-afternoon when Rory swung his car off the main highway. The road from Cape Town had been virtually free of traffic and for some two hundred kilometres or so we had only seen one or two petrol tankers and the occasional heavy transporter.

'That must be the Clanwilliam Dam,' I said as my eyes caught a sparkle of water in the bright afternoon sun.

'Look behind you and you will see the dam wall,' said Rory as we headed towards the small town of Clanwilliam. 'Not too far to go now.'

There wasn't a great deal of activity in the main street. That was hardly surprising, as it was early January and many locals would be taking a break at the coast or simply sheltering from the blistering sun. Given that, it was hard to imagine a time when there would ever be much activity in this remote Western Cape settlement.

'Go out on to the main road, turn right, cross the bridge and then take the second right.'

The cheerful, rotund girl in the small general store gave me exact instructions with the surety of one who had spent a lifetime in that majestic mountain region. Rory turned the car around and within a few minutes we were out of town and heading towards my final destination. It was a matter of moments before the smooth paved road that had been with us throughout the day gave way to the rough grit surface so familiar to those who have travelled throughout Africa. My mind went back forty years to the days when I had travelled for hundreds of miles in East Africa on roads such as this. Then, no insulation would keep the red dust from penetrating every corner of the car. At the end of a journey we would emerge streaked with sweat and covered with grime. Here, in South Africa, the road was firmly packed and well graded. Rory also had a car that was a vast improvement on the vehicles that had taken me on my youthful travels.

We travelled in silence along the valley road. Around us massive craggy peaks bit into the bright blue sky.

We drove deeper and deeper into the mountains, passing whitewashed thatched cottages that would not have looked out of place in the English countryside.

'There it is,' exclaimed Rory suddenly. He pointed to a rough wooden sign where the road divided. 'Dwarsrivier. That's the place, isn't it?'

It was. This was the spot that was to be my place of self-imposed exile for the next several weeks.

I climbed out of the front seat and strolled across the grass to the door of the farmhouse. 'Anyone at home?' I shouted.

Someone responded from within the dark, cool interior and a lady appeared. 'Ah,' she said. 'Glad you could make it and good to see you again. I'll just get the keys and be with you in a moment.' She disappeared and I looked around at the compound. It was as I remembered it.

I first discovered this remote spot when I was asked to join a group of trekkers who were hiking through the Cederberg range of mountains and in the process raising money to support South African children who had fallen victim to HIV infection. I joined them for their first stop at the farm, spent the night under canvas and then returned to Cape Town while they continued their trek through the mountains. It was then that I decided to return one day.

Meanwhile, I had discovered that the farm at Dwarsrivier had a recorded history that went back to the very earliest of the first European settlers. They quickly learned how to harvest the indigenous rooibos tea, which grew freely on the mountain slopes. Gradually they discovered that the area was ideal for a different type of crop, and today this small mountain valley farm, amply watered by two rivers and their swift-flowing tributaries, is an abundant provider of oranges and lemons for the export market.

Therese, the farmer's wife, returned with the keys. 'You're staying in *Oorkant se Huis*,' she said. 'In English that means "The House Over Yonder".' She indicated towards a thatched cottage just visible through the trees. 'It's only a short walk, but as you have luggage, you'd better follow the bakkie in your car. It's a long way round, as we have to go out on to the main track again.'

She jumped into a four-wheel drive and we followed her out on to the track and then on to a smaller trail until we reached the thatched house.

'Well,' said Rory, after we had been given a quick tour of inspection and had humped my luggage out of the boot, 'I hope you're going to be settled here on your own. If you want to come back to Cape Town, there's always a room in our house. I'll get someone to come and collect you.'

Rory is the most generous of friends and I knew his offer was sincerely made. However, I had long ago made up my mind that I needed to return here for some weeks. I needed to be alone. Not simply to write, as I intended, but also to enjoy some solitude.

'Remember I spent many years totally alone in Beirut,' I replied. 'The situation was far worse than this, I can tell you.'

'You'll need a more comfortable seat than that,' he said, pointing to a high wooden stool standing against the only large table available for writing. 'You ought to see if you can buy one in town.'

I nodded, but knew that I wouldn't. I was sure that if necessary Therese would provide something from the main house. We walked outside. Before us stood the jagged formation of the Krakadouw Peak. In the near distance the gentle sound of running water indicated that the house was but a short walk from a stream. Rory climbed back into his car.

'See you in a few weeks, Tel,' he said.

He was returning to Cape Town and after a few days was travelling to the Economic Summit in Davos, Switzerland. I didn't envy him. I watched him disappear down the dusty track until I could hear the sound of the car engine no longer. Then I turned and faced the peak.

What secrets do you hold? I said to myself, as I gazed at the solid jagged rock. *I wonder what secrets are held in this solitary place.*

The house was all on one level and was totally suitable for my needs. Admittedly I could have done with more comfortable writing facilities, but apart from that it was fine. I lugged my heavy suitcase through to the main bedroom and began to unpack.

Although I have been travelling for well over forty years, I have yet to learn the art of travelling light. I can only imagine that some deep inner insecurity compels me to pack far more than I actually need.

Once everything was in place, I took a look around. In a small bookcase built into the wall of the living room, there were six books: three with red covers and three with black. Closer inspection revealed that they were *Reader's Digest* condensed editions. I doubted that I would open them, as I had brought a reasonable supply of books with me. The kitchen area was attached to the living room. The fridge was new and spacious. The two-ring hotplate cooker was small but adequate. There was hot water, and a look at the bathroom revealed there was a full-length bath and a shower. Sheer luxury. In the bedroom I lay out on the double bed and discovered it was plenty long enough for my six-foot-seven frame. Above me were rough wooden rafters, and above them plain reed thatch. I remembered reading that old-fashioned four-poster beds normally had a canopy over them in order to prevent mice and other creatures from dropping from the rafters on to the slumbering occupants below. I had yet to see a mouse, although I had spotted several very large spiders, towards which I felt well disposed, as they would deal with flying insects instantly.

As I got up from the bed, my eye caught sight of a black-and-white drawing. It seemed odd. It portrayed what appeared to be a couple of Nissen-type huts, a watchtower and what seemed like a perimeter fence. Was it some form of prison camp?

In the early evening Therese came across to see that everything was in order and I asked her about the picture.

'I bought it some time ago at an auction,' she said. 'It held a strange fascination for me and I wondered if it represented the concentration camp that was set up in this area during the Boer War. There was a camp on the edge of Clanwilliam. My grandfather told me that British soldiers were stationed here on this farm. When you walk across to the farm-house, cross the stream and before you cross the dried-up riverbed, look at one of the rocks on your left. You'll see that someone has carved initials on to it in old script. I got the university people to look at it once and they told me it was probably carved by one of the British soldiers who were stationed here during the war years. There was some sort of army camp on that very spot.'

In the cool of the evening I took a short walk across the stream and into the parched meadow. I found the long flat stone easily enough and there, just as Therese had said, were the initials DHM. I examined the other stones in the area, but they were blank. Only this one was marked. Naturally I wondered who DHM was and if there was anyone who held the clue to his or her identity.

The Boer War was a terrible and futile event, and probably one of the first times the British Army had to deal with guerrilla tactics. The Boer farmers refused to stand and fight in the traditional manner the British were accustomed to. They grouped, regrouped, sniped at and completely baffled their regimented enemy. In order to try and prevent the Boers from receiving support from their families and neighbours, camps were set up for women and children, who were forcibly removed from their farms and cottages. The picture in my bedroom was almost certainly one such camp. Conditions were dreadful and thousands died of disease brought on by neglect. The South African war was not one of the most glorious moments in British history.

*

Before leaving Cape Town, I had bought some provisions for the first few days of my stay. I needed to get my body into shape, so I had bought plenty of fruit and vegetables and tins of salmon and tuna fish. I had been told that someone from the farm went into town several times a week and they would either get what I needed or I could go along myself. I opened a small tin of tuna fish, prepared a salad and took it out on to the veranda.

The sun was setting and the mountains were full of soft colours with gentle shading. At times they glowed warm and pink and then as the sun gradually disappeared they changed their tone to a deeper hue. The rock was predominantly Cape sandstone and that, together with the sandy soil, indicated that in prehistoric days the sea had covered this very spot. As I was near the river, plenty of green bushes and trees were visible. Further away from the water, the grass was yellow and withered, and the soil was as sandy as any Cape Town beach.

It takes time to enter into, and enjoy, solitude. Many people have said to me that there had been times when they longed to get away from the turmoil of life and enjoy some peace. When they finally did so, they discovered that, although they may have chosen the most wonderful location, they could not settle. Even in the most idyllic surroundings, solitude can be oppressive. Perhaps one reason for this is because solitude is not so much to do with location; it is more a state of mind. Here, on my first evening alone, I felt some apprehension. The previous year, when I had said farewell to the trekkers and returned to London, I knew that I must, and would, return to the Cederbergs.

In the past I had spent many years in enforced solitude and had had to learn how to cope with the loss of most of the things that were dear to me. When, after almost five years, I was released and returned to my family and friends, I recognized then that the years spent alone had not been wasted. Out of necessity I had become more centred as a person. I had been forced to use my imagination in a disciplined way. I had had to re-sort my priorities in life and, at the same time, discover how to take the experience of isolation and use it creatively. The years as a captive had proved to be a hard school and, without knowing it, I had learned many things, but even today I continue to attempt to understand the experience more completely.

I sat on the small concrete veranda remembering the past until the sun had gone and I could no longer see the mountains. All was still apart from the soothing music of the stream and the sound of a gentle breeze in the trees. I went indoors, prepared my bed, and took another look at the picture of the camp above it. Strangely appropriate, I thought, as I drifted into sleep. Strangely appropriate.

*

I hardly moved from the cool of the house during the first two days. To begin with I sorted out the books I had brought with me. There was a large new biography of Byron, several travel books and a complex book on time that I was reading for the third time. It was written by a physicist with the non-specialist in mind, but as I have no training whatsoever in physics I struggled to understand it; nevertheless, the subject was totally absorbing. My shortwave radio worked perfectly and to my delight I could receive clearly the BBC's World Service. Alas, the news was so depressing that I kept it turned off for most of the time. Each news bulletin contained information about war and the preparations being made for war with Iraq. The world of international relations is a moral mess and from my remote retreat it seemed that elaborate games were being played out on the world stage. What saddens me so much is that the main victims of warfare are invariably innocent women and children. Once the war is over and the combatants have returned home, shattered lives remain behind and there are few to help them. I am convinced that warfare today is an admission of failure.

During the first few days of being alone for some weeks, I knew that I must find some structure for the day. For the first period of captivity in Beirut I was kept underground, often without any light whatsoever, which was disturbing to say the least. Frequently I would awake and imagine that it was time for breakfast, only to discover later that it was the middle of the night. That experience told me how important it is, in such circumstances, to work out a simple structure for the day. It need not be applied rigorously, but a structure is important.

After two or three days in the cottage, I developed a pattern suitable for my needs. I breakfasted at eight on the veranda, looking out towards the mountains. There I traced the shape of their rugged structure and pictures formed in my mind. I saw a face or a reclining figure, and at other times, when the light had changed, a whole new scene was set before me. The morning was given to reading and writing. Rory had been correct when he pointed out that the stool would not be suitable, and I moved my position to sit before a low table brought over by Therese from the main house. Lunch was at midday and at one o'clock I tuned in to the BBC World News and news about the UK. The afternoons were extremely hot, so I slept, usually very soundly. At first I slept for well over two hours, but that was probably because I was still getting acclimatized to the weather. When I had left London it was freezing and getting colder. My evening meal was at six and I was normally in bed by ten. This pattern did not enslave me and I felt quite free to change it whenever I needed to. I also recognized, very clearly, that the one thing sadly missing was exercise. In Beirut, although I was chained for most of the time, I found it absolutely necessary to exercise in whatever way I could. Here in the Cederbergs, I told myself it was too hot, and indeed it was hot, but at root I think I was being lazy. I did, however, determine to include a short walk each evening before the light went.

Compared to my experience of solitary confinement, the house was marvellous. In captivity I had had virtually nothing apart from what I could draw from my experience and shape with my imagination. Now, although I was physically alone, I did not feel totally alone. I was rooted in my family, with my friends, and in my own culture. All these were then physically distant from me, but I was deeply conscious that I *belonged* to all of them and that belonging was mutual. I was fortunate to have a reasonable security in my identity that had been forged through a variety of relationships, and those relationships did not cease when I was physically isolated from them. As for my faith, it enabled me to put my seemingly insignificant, and certainly restricted, life into a much larger context.

Rowan Williams, when he had recently been elected as Archbishop of Canterbury, pointed out in an address how important it was for men and women to be able to place their individual lives within the context of a much greater story. He said that religion enables us to do that. If solitude is to be a creative experience, then it is certainly helpful, if not vital, to be able to recognize that we are not alone. We are deeply related to this world and all that is in it, and specifically related to groups and individuals who enable us to have identity. As we are drawn by 'the Great Story', our identity develops and we find meaning for our personal existence. The religious story, brought alive by faith, gives meaning to some who possess that gift, just as political ideologies give meaning to others.

During the days spent in solitary confinement, I often told myself stories. Some were autobiographical, others were imaginary. I directed my inner voice to follow certain themes; to create characters and, at times, to converse with them. Although I had no pencil and paper, I used to 'write' in my head and this activity kept my mind vigorous and alive. A similar process took place in South Africa. My mind went back across the past ten years of freedom, particularly remembering journeys I had made to discover how other people approached solitude. Then I had pen and paper, and made notes. This place in the mountains was an ideal place to stop and remember for a moment. One of the books I had been reading was the enigmatically titled *The Man Who Mistook His Wife for a Hat* by Oliver Sacks. He quotes from Luis Buñuel, and his remarks seemed to me to be particularly appropriate at this time:

> You have to begin to lose your memory, if only in bits and pieces, to realize that memory is what makes our lives. Life without memory is no life at all . . . Our memory is our coherence, our reason, our feeling, even our action. Without it, we are nothing . . .

One afternoon, when I went over to the farmhouse to catch my ride into town, Pierre, the husband of Therese, was there, as were their two attractive teenage daughters. Pierre is a cheerful, stocky man and has been at this farm for over twenty years. They are an enterprising family. They have harnessed the power of the sun, and a solar panel at the side of the farmhouse provides them with their abundant hot water. The clean, sweet water I was drinking is drawn directly from the river, and irrigation pipes enable the sandy pastures to produce grass even at the hottest time of the year.

During the drive into Clanwilliam, Therese told me that there are leopards in the mountains behind the cottage, but as they are such shy animals, they are seldom seen. They rarely cause trouble. Once a mother with three cubs took a couple of sheep from the farm, but rather than shoot the leopard, which would have been illegal, Pierre moved the sheep to a safer location. Some time ago a survey was made and, after a period of decline, the leopard population was discovered to be on the increase.

She told me about a new calf that had quite a short tail. 'It's possible that a leopard snapped at it,' she said. 'When the cows are in the field by your cottage, notice how close the calf stays by her mother. She protects her and probably protected her from the leopard.'

For several mornings the cooing of a dove outside my bedroom window awakened me. I wouldn't have minded a short burst, but this bird had amazing powers of endurance, and continued for hour after hour. One day it returned mid-morning and I chased it away from the eaves of the house. I was somewhat ashamed about moving on a dove, of all birds, but this was a very noisy dove! I suspected that this would not be the last I'd see of it. The Cederbergs are a haven for wildlife, particularly birds. I enjoyed watching them in the early morning and again in the evening, but I encouraged the dove to keep its distance!

The days in Clanwilliam passed pleasantly enough. The weather was perfect and at no time was I disturbed by intrusions from the world outside my own small world. However, something was not right. I tried to read, but my concentration wandered. I sat at the small table with a blank notepad before me, but no inspiration came. I grew increasingly anxious. Here I was in the most perfect of surroundings and yet totally unable to make creative use of the time. Now I was experiencing what I had experienced prior to captivity, when I had been advised to leave work for a day or so and go into retreat. I had vivid recollections of those days when I was restless and ill at ease with myself and the surrounding situation. Now, that experience was being repeated in South Africa, and I was profoundly disappointed.

It was with very mixed feelings that I received Rory when he came to collect me at the end of my stay.

'Well, Tel,' he said, in his usual cheery manner, 'have you written much?'

I wasn't totally honest with him and muttered something about it being a useful time to get away for reflection. I did not say that I had written virtually nothing and was returning to the UK empty-handed.

*

In putting the various experiences of solitude together to form this book, I debated with myself whether to include this chapter on Clanwilliam. I decided I would, as it illustrates another aspect of solitude: the fact that it can be a dry and frustrating time. To make creative use of the experience, one needs to have reasonably clear goals about what one wishes to get from the time set apart. At that time, ideas were buzzing about in my head but I had no clear understanding of what I wanted to write. Try as I might, I could not get clarity, nor enough inner peace, to reflect calmly. It was a hard time, especially as I had fondly imagined that my years alone had equipped me for the experience. I was located in a solitary place, but inwardly I was not connecting with it. It was many years later that I came to the recognition that in Clanwilliam the ideas for future writings were still to be developed and I needed to have patience.

Some time later I wrote the following Songs of Solitude, which were set to music and performed in Norwich Cathedral.

At night, I often sit for a while and gaze into the heavens. In this vast, solitary space, my own existence seems inconsequential. Around me, the world as I know it continues on its own troubled way. In the heavens, the chains of time that bind me to the earth are loosed. The distances are immeasurable. Across the years mankind has looked heavenwards for release from the burdens of life; for eternal peace, for rest. Little wonder that the psalmist could declare that the heavens proclaimed the glory of God, and the supreme being was to be found in the still, small voice. One does not have to be religious to experience the wonder of solitude. Religion provides an interpretation that may be accepted or rejected.

Solitude is a fact. It is within us, and around us, and has the power to create awe and wonder or to lead us into utter despair. It is an integral part of the human condition and of the universe of which we are a part. Solitude pre-exists us, accompanies us, and continues long after our mortal remains return to the dust from whence they came. Solitude is a song of life, of death, of eternity. It exists within the depths of a soul and in the vastness of space. It is the source of harmony and wholeness. It is my song. It is your song.

SONGS OF SOLITUDE

My song is a song of solitude.
My voice sings across the years;
   echoes down the corridors
   of memory; ebbs and flows
   across the shores of the
   unconscious.

My song is the song of a child.
   A plaintive, hungry child.

My song is the song of the grave.
A lament.

My song is maternal, paternal and filial.

My song has no beginning. No ending.

In the formless waste and void my song stirred
across the face of the waters.

In the pulsing, urban cacophony my song shook the
earth.

My song lingers in the prisons: drifts through the
valleys and saunters through the byways of night.
My song is a piercing cry that divides flesh from
spirit.
My song is a healing balm that consoles and heals.
My song has many words and no words, many
voices and no voices.
My song travels with the pilgrim and rests with the
wounded.

My song is your song.
Your song is my song.

We sing alone.
We sing together.
Our melody knows no bounds.

We sing to the music of time.
We sing to the music of eternity.

We lament.
We rejoice.

Our song is the song of solitude.
Our song is the song of life.

My song is the song of a child

Childhood is a memory
That lingers in the mind
With gentle sadness.

The empty darkness of night
When shadows shape the blackness
And whisper the language of the lost.

The scorching heat of day;
A day without end.
No past – no future.

I hold my mother's hand
As we tread the endless corridor of time.
Soon it will be night.
Soon we will be shadows in memory.

Times past – times present.
My song is timeless.

In the byways of memory
The child is the man – the man is the child.
The shadows give shape to blackness.
My song lingers in memory.

My song is the song of the grave

You tread softly
With sureness of foot.
Gently waiting your time.

When man stirred from dust
You were there.
When ashes were strewn
You were there.

Behind the tear
Concealed by the smiles
You wait.

The solitary embrace of death enfolds us,
Life departs and life is given.
Beyond the broken fragments of time
A flower blooms.
Beyond the laments the gentle melody of death.

My song is maternal, paternal and filial

Your faces are one.
Your one face is many.

You are mother.
Troubled compassion sleeps in your eyes.
You are father,
Surrounded and alone,
Ever seeking to heal inner loneliness of soul.
You are son, daughter, brother, sister –
Many and yet one.

The one is in the many;
The many are in the one.
You sing alone – you sing in chorus,
From the eternal music of solitude.

In the pulsing, urban cacophony my song shook the earth

The words are hard.
They echo with the timbre of brutality.
Their colour is grey;
The greyness is concrete.
Their song is harsh –
A harshness that covers the earth with stone
And entombs the spirits for ever.

I walk through lonely streets.
No grass.
No sky.

'This place is for profit, sir. We must have jobs.'
A young girl weeps alone.

'This place is for pleasure, sir. We all have our little
     indulgences.'
A man with the eyes of a terrified animal drinks
     deeply from a bottle.

'We need to forget, sir. From time to time, that is.
    We need to forget.'
No one asks what is to be forgotten.
And why.

My song is a piercing cry

I see the wisdom of the ages in your troubled face.
Abraham, Isaac and Jacob.
You tell me you know them not.
But they know you.

'My father was a stranger to me.'
All your fathers were distant,
And you embraced them not.
But they embraced you.

The Kindertrain is waiting.
Say goodbye to Grandmother.
'Be careful, boy. Take care.'
'Old lady, I love you. Don't leave me alone.'
You embraced.

Along the corridor of time you lie alone.
Pain stalks your troubled body.
Yesterday is with you now.
The same train – the same grandmother – the same
    forefathers.
Now you may cry the bitter tears of anguish.
Now you may howl with the primitive howl of a lost
    soul.
Now you may embrace . . . for ever.

The cry that tore soul from body,
Kith from kin,
Is now a song.

'By the waters of Babylon we sat down and wept.'
We also drank.

My song is a healing balm that consoles and heals

A melody may please.
A tune may delight.

A healing song will hurt.

Within it is the music of eternity.

Part 2

DECEPTIVE SOLITUDE

During a prolonged period of solitude, one experiences time differently from the way it is experienced in normal life. It is not easy to describe how this feels. Living without familiar reference points can produce a dream-like state where life is lived almost completely within the imagination. Now, as I look back on the years I spent totally alone, they seem to have passed in a flash. In my memory, one day has melted into another. At the time, I was acutely conscious of the importance of memory and of that which I described as the past. It was as though the past, and those who inhabited it, were a part of the experience of the moment.

In this book, I am repeating something of what I did when I was alone. I am sauntering through solitude. I like that word. The Oxford dictionary suggests connotations of idleness, even of purposelessness. For me, when I saunter I move through experiences, stopping where I will, savouring the moment before moving on. I like to saunter. In solitude I spent long hours sauntering through my past life, recalling the people and places I had known. My mind frequently returned to Africa, where I had my first overseas posting.

In the days before General Amin, the British expatriate community in Uganda was quite small, but the major countries of the world had their diplomatic representations, and the UK, because of its long-standing involvement with the country, was prominent. Our children went to the local international school and it was from this experience that they developed a sympathy and understanding of other cultures that formed and shaped their lives. Like expatriate children the world over, birthday parties figured high on their list of social activities. There was one occasion, I remember, when they had attended a school party. Afterwards, parents were invited in for a drink before driving their charges home. One parent, a first secretary in a foreign embassy, stood outside with a brand-new camera. First, his own daughter appeared and he took her photograph. Then several other children emerged with their parents. He insisted that he should be given an opportunity to use his new camera and take their photographs also. Within twenty minutes he had photographed every parent and child at the party and had promised to let everyone who wanted one have a copy. My companion smiled. 'Clever,' he said. 'In a few short minutes he has completely updated his photographic record of most of the important businessmen and others in Kampala.' Later, I learned that the genial First Secretary was in the employ of his country's intelligence service.

I thought of that trivial incident when I went to have a conversation with a friend of mine who had served in British Intelligence for some twenty-five years of his career. I suggested that we meet during a weekday morning in London. I was interested not so much in the operational detail that had engaged him during his service, but in the effect this unusual form of solitary life had had on him.

Exactly on the hour my friend arrived. He made his way to where I was seated. We settled ourselves down and ordered coffee. I had previously explained the reasons why I wanted to have a discussion with him, but by way of settling in I told him of my travels so far. I mentioned the Australian outback, the visit to Chicago and the casual, almost inconsequential, visit to Solitude. As he began to speak, I listened carefully.

On the occasions we had met previously I had noticed the precision with which he spoke. The way in which he measured his words spoke of a lifetime of guarded conversation. And yet his whole manner was relaxed, low key, exactly what one would expect from one who, despite inner anxieties, had had to maintain a polite, almost bland exterior.

He began by deprecating himself, deliberately underplaying his suitability as a subject for discussion. He had never lived under 'deep cover'. Through his experience in the service he had met with many people who had lived a totally secret life abroad. He had seen at first hand the strain that this imposed on individuals, and recognized that they were required to lead lives of total solitude. He compared these situations with his own. Living as he had done under 'shallow cover' was somewhat less stressful. He had joined the Intelligence Branch when he was in his thirties and married with young children, and was able to share the fact with his wife.

'It's a matter of discretion,' he said. 'You can hardly expect your wife to live with a lie and not realize it's a lie.'

He had acquired his fascination for intelligence during his time as a District Officer in the Colonial Service.

'I recognized that the work went beyond the ordinary scope of diplomacy. It was the acquisition of information for the good of the government by means other than overt techniques. In the straight Foreign Service you enter and learn the job as you go along. In the Intelligence Service, initially you are sent away for a period of residential training, which does have its James Bondish side. Weapons training, that sort of thing. But the reality is far from that which is presented in popular novels. Those living under deep cover do face very considerable strain, particularly as you know any breach, or indiscretion, can cause the loss of somebody's life. Not your own, probably – in fact almost certainly not your own – but perhaps the life of the agent with whom you are in touch. It means that you are walking a tightrope all the time, because you can't afford to let up or relax. It's terribly easy to forget. There was a time when I was taking part in an exercise in London and was required to live an alias. I checked in at a London hotel and the receptionist asked me to sign a sheet of paper. I signed my own name instead of the alias. My attention had slipped for a moment. Fortunately I was able to remedy that. By a stroke of luck the receptionist was distracted for a minute and I was able to snatch another sheet and fill it in with my allotted cover name. But that was a thing one never forgets: the ease with which one can drop out of pretence into reality. That forgetful moment may be fatal to somebody.'

During the course of his varied career, my friend had lived under shallow cover in many different parts of the world. He had an extraordinary ability to learn foreign languages quickly. Within three or four weeks, he would be able to both write and speak a new European language, and in his lifetime had mastered 'hard', non-European languages, some six or seven in all. His first posting was as a First Secretary abroad.

'The number of people who were aware that I was in the Intelligence Branch had to be limited to the absolute minimum. I constantly had to refer to myself as being what I wasn't: a member of the straight branch. It did involve a certain amount of loneliness – which was certainly mitigated by the fact that my wife was in the picture from the start – but there are all sorts of social questions that arise. Why aren't you free at the weekend, when the embassy is known to be unoccupied by something prevailing at the moment such as a royal visit? Where have you gone to when you are meeting somebody at a remote place? You have to invent stories. You have to lie. I suppose I quite enjoyed lying, because it was in a good cause and didn't involve personal corruption, but it does impose a strain.'

My mind strayed to the various agents I had known during my life. You knew that they would lie. It was a part of their stock-in-trade. And yes, there had to be some degree of mutual trust. The problem was that the relationship was based on suspicion, even if you were meeting those who belonged to so-called friendly services.

'Does telling lies have a corrupting effect on individuals?' I asked.

My friend pondered for a moment and then answered in his careful manner. 'I think it can. I can't immediately remember people of whom I thought this, but you get so used to telling lies about who you are and what you are doing that it could warp your character to some extent. The fact that I can't identify that in myself may be an indication that I have been corrupted by it. I don't know. I don't think it's a very serious factor, though. What you had to do all the time was to stick as closely to the truth as possible. If you were going somewhere to meet somebody, it was as well to have a genuine purpose as well as a clandestine one. It diminished the sense of surprise if you were seen by people somewhere you had a good reason to be. It took a lot of hard work to organize that.'

There was a gentle knock on the door and our coffee arrived. I poured two cups and added a touch of milk. One sugar for my friend, none for myself. We remained silent for a while. It wasn't an uneasy, tense silence – more of a reflective relaxed space within which there was an opportunity to consider that which had passed between us. Earlier we had discussed the qualities required by a good intelligence officer. My friend had singled out several: good at languages, interested in and sympathetic towards people, able to be a soft shoulder for people to lean on. It was necessary, he said, to have an empathy with disparate kinds of people and it certainly wasn't a job for a self-centred, personally ambitious or routine-minded person. It was a job for the exception rather than the rule. A first-class degree was not a necessary requirement and it was difficult to be exact as to what was required. Most had something unusual to offer that was not easy to describe.

We drank our coffee slowly.

'Of course,' said my friend, as he pushed his cup and saucer to one side, 'one of the menaces in British Intelligence work abroad is the British community. They do not take it seriously. I can remember all sorts of instances where my cover, such as it was, was threatened.'

'Can you give me an example?' I asked.

'Well, first of all I should say that there was no ill-will. It was more a matter of sheer ignorance and the dramatic-mindedness of one's British

The open flatlands near Cloncurry, Queensland

A pilot with Jacqui and Bruce Farrands in Rabbit Flat,
Northern Territory

A pilot and Terry Waite with Terry and John Underwood in Riveren, Northern Territory

Terry being pulled along the River Humbert, Northern Territory

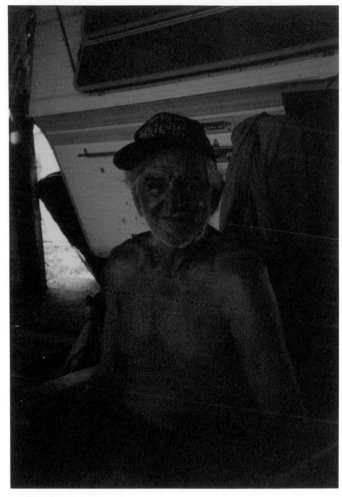

Station worker Ronnie at Humbert River Station,
Northern Territory

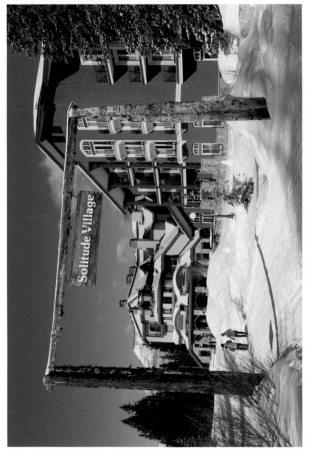

The gate to the main square of Solitude Village, Utah

Terry with George Blake in Moscow, Russia, 2001.

Myra Hindley, who was convicted with Ian Brady for the Moors Murders in the 1960s

Svetlana Stalin, daughter of Joseph Stalin

Harold Lock, who was held in a Japanese prisoner-of-war camp, 1942–5

colleagues abroad, who saw it all as an adventure. To them, James Bond or Sexton Blake was the scene and they found it all very exciting. If they had been in the picture as to what one was doing, they would have found it very difficult to keep their mouths shut, because they had been brought up in quite different conditions from those that prevailed in Eastern Europe, where the world of intelligence, or KGB, or whatever it might be, was synonymous with threat, danger or death; the knock on the door in the small hours of the night. In a freer society such as our own, the average citizen has no idea at all, apart from reading novels or seeing films, of the lives of those in the secret services. On the other hand, one is glad to belong to a society where this is the situation rather than sinister menace.'

My friend took one of his characteristic pauses and I pushed the coffee pot in his direction. He half filled his cup and resumed his story.

'Once, in Africa, I was at a party when one of my contacts, who was aware of what I was doing, came up and said, "How do you do?" in a polite way, as though he hardly knew me, which was good of him. Someone else came up and said, "Oh, what do you do in the High Commission?" I was about to embark on my cover story, which was that I was on the political staff of the High Commissioner as a First Secretary, when my contact interrupted me with a savage look and said, "Shut up! Go away – don't ask these questions." It was grotesquely inapposite and threw me completely. Most people have had that sort of experience with the British community abroad.'

Again he paused, as in his mind he reflected on his African days. I pondered on the strangeness of the intelligence sub-culture. Every embassy and High Commission had such people on the staff and more often than not they all knew each other. In turn they gleaned what they could from their contacts and provided a modest income for a very few local agents. From past experience, I knew how very difficult it could be for anyone on the staff of an embassy to win the confidence of local people even if, as in the case of my friend, they had taken the trouble to learn obscure tribal languages.

My friend turned his thoughts to his position within the Foreign Office hierarchy.

'Living under even a shallow degree of cover did mean that I became a bit of a misfit. For instance, as I grew older and more senior, the question would arise as to why I wasn't a High Commissioner or an ambassador, and old friends wondered if I had done something wrong. In fact, I was as senior and well paid as many High Commissioners and ambassadors, but without the tinsel that went with it. I was lucky. I picked up decorations, deserved or not, but I picked them up, which in some sense mitigated that experience, but I still meet people who say, "It's funny you were never an ambassador." From the point of view of one's family, as the children grew up there was a marked difference of status. "There goes the humble First Secretary . . ." Which of course wasn't one's real rank but a cover rank. Their friends' parents were obviously doing much better. One had to live with a certain amount of humility in that respect.'

I asked him if he was able to tell his children the real nature of his work.

'Yes, when they reached the age of discretion, which I took to be middle teens. I told them each, one by one, and I had their total cooperation and trust. They took it very well. They had seen that I was happy, and calculated that it was something worthwhile I was doing.'

My friend continued to discuss the Foreign Office hierarchy.

'One of the ablest intelligence officers I ever knew never got beyond the rank of First Secretary, although he was paid several grades higher than that. In order to fit into a small embassy or High Commission, he had to accept a lowlier rank. The Foreign Office is a rank-conscious organization and those who are unaware of the reality tend to think that one must have made an awful flop somewhere to be so held back in one's career. Of course, as you get older you become more exposed and are noted on all sorts of lists as a likely or certain intelligence officer. Then it's possible to be a little franker with more distant relatives.'

I told my friend that I would be interested to hear what he had to say about the pressures put upon his family as a result of his chosen occupation. In the days when I was dealing with situations of extreme sensitivity I did not discuss my work at all with my wife. I felt that it would be unfair to subject her to extra pressures. I did need to share with someone, however, so I did share with one or two trusted friends or colleagues. Even then I could not share everything and I found the pressures exceptionally hard to deal with. Unlike my friend, I did not have the support of an organization that he had.

He began his comments by referring back to the question of status. 'Very often there is pressure from the wife for her husband to get out of something where she is looked down on in status by people who are younger than her. Then there is what is perceived as the unfairness of it. To act as backstop in a game where she can't participate operationally, she is expected to keep her mouth shut and to keep telling lies, which she is not accustomed to and not trained to do. This can cause considerable stress, resulting in resignation, if not divorce. There is a high rate of divorce in the Intelligence Branch, as there is in the Foreign Office generally. I would say, though, that the Intelligence Branch is the happier because it is more of a clique, more of a club and, of course, a smaller unit. The wives on the whole are marvellous, and of course when I say that today, I should also include the husbands. As for alcoholism, well, I have not come across many serious drunks in my service career and I certainly never came across more in my branch. The cocktail circuit is somewhat overwritten. It does exist, but it's not so much a way of life as it's made out to be. I can't honestly recall more than one or two people who were seriously alcoholic.'

We discussed what I call compartmentalism: the living of life in different compartments, occasioned in my friend's case by having to practise deception. Did it inhibit his own growth towards greater wholeness as a person?

He answered without any hesitation. 'No. I don't think one is any less whole. In fact one may be more so, as one has had to think harder. It's an unrelated life. Always one has to bear in mind the possibility of betrayal, misunderstanding or exposure. I don't think that makes one any less of a whole person. I do think that the personality benefits from strain and stress, of which there is a considerable amount.'

I said that I supposed the key lies in each individual being able to know what is an acceptable level of stress for him or her and being properly supported through periods of exceptional stress. I asked my friend if he had ever been betrayed. He said that he had never been in a position where any of his agents were likely to get shot. His final postings reflected the seniority of his position and he occupied a liaison function with foreign intelligence services. He had been taken for a ride during his career and there were many people who turned out to be what he described as 'flops'. There were those who disappeared after promising to make themselves available. He could understand that. There were many disappointments. He had known a number of individuals who had been interrogated by hostile services and had given way. Afterwards they had had to pull out, or in some cases had been sacked. Looking back on his career, my friend said that he would certainly do the same job again.

'Right up to the end, I found that my job was more interesting than if I had been in the straight Foreign Service. You were on the inside track dealing with truths and factors that didn't hit the news and were not going to be reported, but which you knew to be true. You had responsibility beyond your age and rank. If you can imagine the responsibility of somebody sent out to a remote place, under deep cover, running a one-man or one-woman station. He may be a twenty-five-year-old, surrounded by people old enough to be his parents, and yet he has his particular responsibilities that he can share with nobody, not even his secretary – if he has one. He has his own codes and ciphers, his own room, his own briefing, his own mission to accomplish, or fail to accomplish. He has nobody immediately at hand to share that responsibility, unlike his regular colleagues, who can lean on each other.

'It was a lonely life, but it repaid itself because of the degree of responsibility you got far beyond your age or your declared rank.'

Although our conversation was drawing to a natural end and it was approaching lunchtime, there were many other questions I wanted to ask. First, about the concealment, or holding back, of truth. Did he ever feel that the truth of situations, about which he had inside information, ought to be known? Again he answered immediately. He believed that the truth often did come out in the end – for example, in memoirs and in the disclosure of public documents after the thirty-year rule had expired.

'It's the shorter-term disparity which is more to the point. You know, perhaps, that a situation is worse than, or better than, it appears, but you can't say so and within a year it will all be cleared up. But for a year you are carrying information in your head which you can't divulge, except to your superiors in London by coded signal. And yes, I can recall incidents where I had to keep my mouth firmly shut, because I knew things that ran completely counter to what other people were saying. I couldn't divulge them. That's a strain, but it's one you get used to. It's more difficult the first year or so after joining, but then as the years go by you get more experience.'

Aware that the ethical problems associated with such a stance could only be resolved if the individual concerned maintained an unswerving loyalty to 'My country (and perhaps some other friendly countries), right or wrong', I asked how he viewed morally ambiguous situations within which there was a personal discrediting of an individual for political purposes.

'Yes, that does exist. All I can say is that in over twenty years I never did anything I was ashamed of and I don't look back to anything that I regret. I don't think, for example, that it compares badly with business

procedures. Yes, you are trying to recruit people to provide informa
tion they shouldn't be providing, but you know they are doing the same
to other countries and to your own and this is part of the rules of the
game and what you are paid for. You do your best to protect the person you have recruited, and the whole effort is to the greater good. It's
possible to take an almost Jesuitical approach to this, I think. Certainly
I don't have anything on my conscience about my years in the service. I
might have had if I had been a businessman engaged in industrial
espionage, doing down opponents or bribing my way into contacts.'

'Are recruits taught a code of ethics?'

'Yes, a very strict code of personal and professional conduct. There
must be no falsifying of claims and one must *always* tell the truth to
one's head office. The real sin against the Holy Ghost, so to speak, would
have been to falsify intelligence. That was a resigning matter and an issue
over which you would expect to get the sack. It hardly ever happened and
when it did it was a matter of profound shock. I remember hearing once
that one of my colleagues, widely respected, had invented some information which he passed off as intelligence. I found this appalling. It was
wrong and so rare. He was sacked.'

Finally I asked my friend whether or not he held any religious belief.
His reply was straightforward. He was, if anything, a stoic. An agnostic
and not an atheist.

'What has always put me off about Christianity as a revealed religion
is the bargains it imposes. I feel that to worry too much about one's
soul is somehow demeaning and too egocentric to be appealing ethically.
I think that one should do what one sees to be one's duty and hope for
the best. Personally, I hope there is no afterlife, because to me there is
satisfaction in going out like the flame of a candle. I see no reason at all
to suppose there will be a heaven or a hell.'

We walked to the bar together and had a drink. At lunch we chatted
about matters of mutual interest and then he left to attend a meeting.
Later, I reflected on our conversation. I liked my friend. He was a decent
man who had been able to square his conscience because of his cast-iron
loyalty and concept of duty to his country. He was, in the best sense, one
of the old school. There had been a solitary side to his life, but that side
had been eased by close family ties and a totally supportive organization.
Stress had not worn him down – rather, the reverse. He appeared to have
flourished on it. Although there would have been many who took issue
with him over a number of ethical questions, he had survived because

f the support he had had through his life. I doubted whether he had the *need* to be alone. He was a sociable family man. He certainly had the *capacity* to be alone in a significant area of his life. He seemed to have rather enjoyed his unusual form of solitude. Or perhaps he was just well practised at telling lies.

It was a beautiful morning. The sort of morning I remember from childhood. The sky was cloudless and the wind warm and gentle. Several miles back I had turned off the motorway and now drove gently along a country lane. There were wild flowers in the hedgerow and I could smell freshly mown hay. This was the England that I remembered in times of despair. An England unspoiled by the ravages of urban development, and unchanged since Edwardian times. Ted had given me directions over the telephone.

'You won't miss the house, but if you do, they all know where we live.'

We hadn't previously met. I wanted to meet him in order to continue my discussion on the solitude of the spy. Unlike my previous confidant, who had practised his trade through the ranks of the diplomatic service, Ted had entered into intelligence work through the Armed Forces. Although it was a number of years since he had been active, he had had a colourful career culminating in captivity and torture. Now, deep in the English countryside, he was spending his later years as a solitary writer and caring for an invalid wife.

As predicted, I found the house easily and stopped the engine of the Land Rover. For a moment I remained in my seat and absorbed the silence. Ted had chosen well. Although the summer had been exceptionally dry, the flowers in his garden were in full bloom and the whole picture was one of rural tranquillity. He was waiting for me, casually dressed in blue denim jeans and matching shirt.

We went into the living room, comfortably furnished and lined with books. He introduced me to his foreign-born wife, and as we were drinking coffee one of his daughters arrived. The spontaneous affection she showed towards him told me much about the kind of man Ted was. When we had finished our coffee, Ted stood.

'Come,' he said, 'we'll go and sit in the conservatory.'

I commented on the grapes that were growing everywhere.

Ted smiled. 'I lived in Italy for a while,' he said. 'I was doing a bit of clearing up after the war and had to arrest one chap who lived on the Via Veneto in Rome. He was a very pleasant chap and gave himself up without any difficulty. As we were chatting, he told me he had paid in advance for his flat for a year. He handed me the keys and told me that I might as well use it, together with his car! I did just that and had a wonderful time.'

I could see how it was that, in his later life, Ted Allbeury had become a writer with more than two dozen books to his credit, mainly about espionage. He was a born storyteller with a natural intuition and an excellent sense of humour, although, just like my previous confidant, he began by playing himself down.

'People don't realize that not everyone who works for the Secret Intelligence Service is a James Bond. There are all sorts. Academics, analysts . . . there are so many layers. Before we talk, let me tell you my deal with the old firm. They said that I could write anything I liked, so long as it was fiction. I could put what I had done in story form, but I must not write it as fact.'

This left me with a bit of a problem. It was clear that Ted, being a storyteller, would want to tell me stories. What was I to write? He said that he had experienced a similar problem with the CIA when he was writing about their activities. He had been prepared to submit his manuscript to them before publication and if there was anything in it that endangered individuals, he would remove it. Otherwise he would not allow them to censor it. I said that in my case I was more interested in the solitary aspect of his intelligence life than in operational details. However, I would certainly send him my manuscript and he could make what suggestions he wished. We then settled down under the vines to chat for an hour or so.

We began by talking about *The Times* newspaper. I continued to regret that, some years before, *The Times* had succumbed to the spirit of the age and removed the advertisements from its front page. I had appreciated being able to read the personal column before plunging into the domestic and international news pages. Ted had once read copies of *The Times* in Eardington public library. In the years before the declaration of the Second World War, he had worked as a jig and tool draughtsman in Birmingham. Like so many young men of his generation, he wanted to be a fighter pilot. He passed all the necessary requirements and just as he was about to join up, his job was declared a reserved occupation. The RAF said that in view of this they were unable to accept him.

With all the determination of youth, Ted was not to be put off. He v̇
the recruiting office in James Watt Street, Birmingham, and presen.
himself before an individual whom he described as a 'dear old Evely.
Waugh-type colonel'. The colonel told Ted not to worry about reserved
occupations. A man of Ted's height ought to go into the Guards. Ted
put down for the Guards and within a day or so received a summons to
appear in court, charged with leaving a reserved occupation without permission. He was fined thirty pounds, which was later reduced to fifteen
pounds. Ted now found himself in difficulty. His previous employers
didn't want him back, because if they took him, they wouldn't get a
replacement for him when he eventually left. The Ministry of Labour
didn't want to know him, and the army preferred to wait until the dust
had settled. Ted filled in some spare time at Eardington public library.

'First, I always read the *Times* personal column and was amused at
such items as "Would the girl in the green hat on the train to Sanderstead
like to meet the man smoking a pipe?", that sort of romantic rubbish.
However, there was an ad which interested me. It read, "Linguists
required for special work in the army. Write to box number . . ." Like an
idiot, I wrote to the box number and received a notification to go for an
interview.' Ted had always been interested in languages, and spoke good
German and French. He told me that he got annoyed if he was in a country where he couldn't speak the language.

The interview was conducted in the best of cloak-and-dagger traditions. Ted was to present himself at a barber's shop in London. He was
to ask to see a Mr Waters. Those who asked to see this gentleman were
conducted behind a curtain and up some stairs. Others simply got a
short back and sides.

'There were about eight of us being interviewed. After they had tested
us for language skills, they moved into a different area. The army was
just beginning to get interested in psychiatry and so they gave us the
Rorschach Inkblot test. Then there was this marvellous thing. They pro-
jected six slides on to a screen and we were to write down immediately
what came to mind first. The first slide was a picture of an MG sports
car. The next was a little girl on a swing, and this was followed by a naked
lady lying on a bed with a naked fellow. I remember the psychiatrist saying to me afterwards, "Did you really think that was a nurse attending
the wounded?" This was the time when the army psychiatrists asked
you questions which were supposed to be terribly revealing, but nobody
really knew what a good answer was.

ell, I was accepted and the dear old chap in charge said, "Bring your
orts gear and your car. We'll see that you get some coupons. You're join-
ng a club that will stand you in good stead for the rest of your life, my
boy. You'll have a wonderful time and we'll look after you." This gave me
my first doubts about the service, as they were supposed to have done a
security clearance on me. They were talking about bringing my car, when
I had just spent fifteen shillings on buying my first second-hand bicycle.'

Ted was instructed to go to Winchester and find his training centre, a
former theological college. The initial course was designed for people of
different skills and backgrounds, and the modular structure of the course
meant that individuals could be cut off at certain points or shunted off
in a variety of directions. Some would be trained as linguists for work as
interpreters or in interrogation centres. Ted went to field security. After
Winchester he trod the well-worn route to Smedleys Hydro at Matlock
in Derbyshire, long a centre for training in espionage. Then it was up to
Scotland for commando training. All in all, quite a thorough grounding.

As a training exercise, Ted was given the task of penetrating and
reporting on one of two organizations. They were chosen for exercise
purposes not because of their politics, but because both were controlled
from outside the country. The first was the Jehovah's Witnesses and
the second was the Oxford Group. Ted chose Frank Buchman's Oxford
Group, or Moral Re-Armament to give it its correct title. This movement
was brought to the UK in 1938 by Buchman and was regarded with some
degree of suspicion. One of the practices that caused outsiders to look on
the group with apprehension was group confession of past failings. Ted
was amused by this.

'I remember thinking, when all these beautiful girls stood up and
confessed, what immoral things they had done before they were con-
verted and I was sorry that I hadn't joined earlier.'

Following the exercise, Ted caught sight of his report, on which was
written: 'This is fit only for the *Daily Express*.' In his naivety, he took this
to be a compliment.

As the morning drew on, I realized that we were hardly discussing
solitude in the way I had expected and yet this didn't worry me. Ted had
lived a full and active life. In his latter years he had grown into solitude as
a writer and as a carer for his wife. Now, from his solitude, he was doing
what many solitaries do – tell stories.

Ted's story stirred my own memory. Once, when working for the
release of hostages, I had been introduced to someone who it was

claimed would be helpful to my enquiries. We met on several occasions in London and the individual introduced himself with what was clearly a false name. As is often the case, the individual concerned produced no useful information whatsoever. Several years later, I recognized the photograph of my former contact in a national newspaper. Of course the name given was different from the one I knew, and I looked long and hard before finally deciding that the picture was of the person I knew years ago. Regrettably, he had been found dead in the most horrific circumstances and the full story surrounding his death is still unknown to me. While Ted had an easy, almost casual, way of speaking about past experiences, he knew as well as I that he was speaking of situations that were highly dangerous and often incredibly complex. I remember feeling the isolation of my position. Of being surrounded by deception and double deception. Of never being able to trust anyone. That terrible feeling of vulnerability that grips your stomach and fills you with nausea. Later, you make light of the experience, but at the time it can be deeply disturbing.

Ted's first job was as a supply officer for a firm of ships' outfitters. He would go out to Panamanian (and other neutral) ships with a list of suspects and from time to time brought one or two people in. Then, in no time at all, he was off to a WOSBY (Warrant Office Selection Board) and posted to East Africa with the rank of captain. He went to see his commanding officer.

'Well,' said the CO, 'you're working for those people in London. That I know. You'll be going with General Platt to assist the Emperor of Ethiopia.'

Later, Ted found himself working alongside General Wingate.

'One thing I learned,' he said with a smile. 'Never get too close to heroes. You will get killed and they won't. When I was travelling with Wingate, and there was firing in every direction, he would get down and pray with his old-fashioned alarm clock by his side. A very strange man. When the emperor was back on his throne, it was arranged that there would be a huge assembly in Addis. The mail was to be brought in and on the top of the pile was to be a letter from the king in London, saying, in effect, welcome back to the club. I was designated to open this letter before everyone and hand it to the emperor to read. The whole event was troubled from the start. First, Wingate wanted to ride in on a white horse and there was a lot of disputing because it was said that there were only grey horses available. Eventually a suitable mount was found.

Then we went to the public assembly. The mail was brought in and, as arranged, I picked the top letter from the pile, opened it and handed it to the emperor to read. He received it, read it slowly and paused. He then handed it back to me and said, "You read it." It was a letter from Pickfords, the removal and storage people in Bath, which said, "You owe us a hundred and forty-four pounds, and unless payment is received within seven days your goods will be sold." So I did a sort of "Land of Hope and Glory" thing and made up something. Afterwards, the newly appointed British Minister said, "What utter rubbish." So I told him the story and asked him what he would have said.'

We both laughed heartily. The story was so ludicrous that it had to be true, although earlier we had spoken about the telling of lies.

'Everyone tells lies,' he said confidently. 'That's one of the first things they teach you in the service: everyone lies. In interrogation you must let people talk; let them dig a lot of little holes so that eventually they will fall into one. Then you have them.'

Ted was now well into his storytelling stride. Again, my mind drifted back to the years when I was alone, and I would tell myself stories to bring some colour and humour into a bleak existence. I would blend fact with fiction and not infrequently make myself laugh. I wondered just how much Ted was now doing what I had done then.

'There was one very important task I was given which is difficult to talk about, even now, years later. I was told to try and pick up a certain French businessman, a multi-millionaire who was all over the Yemen, Aden, everywhere. My information was that he was supplying fuel to Japanese mother ships in the Indian Ocean to service Japanese submarines. It was thought that the Emperor of Ethiopia was taking a bit of a backhander from this as well, although that was never proven. So, the attitude in London was, "Do anything you can to get hold of him, but be very careful, because he has more influence than we have. If there is a mess, it's your head that will be at the bottom of the pile." Then, unfortunately, I was rumbled by the Palace Guard and given forty-eight hours to get out of the country. It was very difficult for me to get a message to command. However, eventually they said they would send a plane for me and my replacement would be on board. I handed over to this guy, who seemed pretty sharp, and then left for a neighbouring country. Long after I finished with six [MI6] I returned to my old company and took a position as Sales Director. The chairman had a new secretary and when we met she told me that she had been brought up in Addis. She said her

father often spoke about me and she gave me his name. It was the v
Frenchman I had been chasing years before. She went on to say that f.
was now elderly and was giving a large sum of money to a British university. She wanted to invite me to meet him. I said that I didn't think
he would have a good word to say about me, but she disagreed. So, I
went. At the ceremony this girl came over and invited me to meet her
husband. I walked across to him with my hand out and then I dropped
it in surprise. It was the guy I had handed over to! The guy from MI6.
What better insurance can you have than the guy who is supposed to be
catching you marrying your daughter?'

Most people who reminisce about the war years comment on admin-
istrative confusion. Ted had his own stories. He left Africa and was on his
way to a posting in Burma when he was turned back at Ceylon. It had
been realized that he had fluent German and could be useful elsewhere. It
was while he was running a line-crossing operation that he was captured
and interrogated. I could understand his reluctance to speak about this
episode in his life. Few people who have experienced the humiliation of
torture will talk about it at length. Most victims say that it was worse for
others. Ted said that to me. He was put in a bath of cold water and then
a wet towel was placed over his face so that he could hardly breathe. 'You
make a terrible noise when they do that,' he said. We lapsed into silence,
each of us alone with our own painful memories. To be a victim of torture is to be intensely alone. Intensely frightened. Intensely vulnerable.

'What hurt me more than anything,' he said, 'was that when I escaped
they didn't believe me back at home. They thought I must have done a
deal. That hurt me, and it still does.'

*I know, Ted. I know so well. For a while all goes smoothly and then
suddenly the fragile world in which you are operating falls apart. What
little power you had vanishes like a puff of smoke. Now others show you
what power they have.* For a moment I allowed myself to dwell on the
suspicions that had been directed at myself following my release from
captivity. I knew the hurt of that and it was worse than physical torture
itself.

The painful memory of those years of doubt and disbelief had
brought Ted to reflect on his solitude. 'I used to think that solitude was
an unhappy state. Not so now. Sometimes I go to the village churchyard.
It's just off a quiet pathway. I sit there and look over the fields, and then
look at the dates on the tombstones. I find that comforting. When I see
a tree three or four hundred years old, I shiver. It will be there long after

ave gone from this earth. But really, you can't describe solitude to ayone else. As a carer I have my doubts. I wonder how, and when, it's all going to end. I must admit I often come to the end of my patience, but then I say, "Just get on with it, boy. Just get on with it."'

'To be a traitor you have to belong,' he replied. *'I never belonged.'* He had a Dutch mother and an Egyptian father. His British nationality came through his father, who was given British citizenship.

One of our neighbours in London is a well-known and respected lawyer. Across the years he has taken on board the most unpopular of causes and when we met at one of the committees on which we both sat, he happened to mention that he was pursuing a claim on behalf of George Blake.

Since he was a young man, George Blake had been involved in the intelligence world. He began by working with the resistance movement in Holland and eventually joined the British Intelligence Service where, for many years, he acted as a double agent and in that role supplied the Soviet Union with a vast amount of secret material. He was finally detected and sentenced to forty-two years in prison. Following his imprisonment in, and escape from, Wormwood Scrubs, Blake eventually surfaced in Moscow, where he remained totally silent about his activities. He wrote nothing for publication and refused all interviews. Eventually, in the early nineties, he relented and wrote a book entitled *No Other Choice*. The royalties from the sale of this book in the UK were blocked and thus Blake was deprived of them.

My neighbour had been pursuing this seemingly hopeless case for some time and told me that he needed to visit George in Moscow to discuss progress, or lack of it! As I had never been to Moscow, and more particularly as I was fascinated by the unusual solitary life of a double agent, I asked my friend if I might accompany him and if he thought George might be willing to talk with me. He said that he would fax my request to him. Within a few days a reply was received saying that he would be interested to meet me.

We flew to Moscow on a British Airways flight and landed at Sheremetyevo airport in the middle of a ıeatwave. Moscow was sweltering. Once we had collected our luggage, we avoided the expensive cabs touting for business outside the terminal building and walked a few hundred yards to where we could pick up a coach that would deposit us at the nearest Metro station. To benefit from this inexpensive way of getting into the centre of the city you need to be able to understand the Cyrillic alphabet. Fortunately my friend had done his homework. He accurately identified the correct coach and we were soon on our way to the Rossiya Hotel, situated just outside the walls of the Kremlin. At one time it was the largest hotel in the world, boasting some three thousand rooms. It was later overtaken by the Excalibur in Las Vegas. When I paid a return visit to Moscow in 2006, the Rossiya was being demolished, no doubt causing thousands of cockroaches to seek alternative accommodation!

We had arranged to meet George Blake the following morning outside one of the main entrances to the hotel, the southern entrance. At ten o'clock, on a sweltering hot summer's day, my go-between and I stood in the shade of the massive portico. At ten fifteen he gave me an anxious look.

'I'm sure I said ten,' he said, glancing yet again at his watch. 'It's possible I gave him the wrong directions. Wait here and I'll check.'

He set off to walk to the next lobby entrance, seemingly half a mile away. I watched him disappear around the corner of the building and waited. The minutes ticked by and I wondered just how many clandestine meetings George Blake had engaged in during his long career in espionage. He had agreed to meet me for two reasons that I knew of. First, my lawyer friend who arranged the introduction was his lawyer, and he trusted him. Second, he was given an assurance that I would not distort anything he said when I wrote about him in the future. For my part, I was curious about his professional secret activities, but I was especially interested in his solitary life. It seemed to me that anyone who worked in the field of intelligence had, by virtue of the work they engaged in, to lead a double life. I also imagined that this might have a certain solitary aspect to it and it was this I wanted to explore. Several more minutes passed and then in the distance I spotted my companion. He was accompanied by a man of medium height and as they came nearer I could see that he was smartly dressed, bearded, and that he walked with a slight limp. He approached and held out his hand.

'Good morning, Mr Waite. I'm sorry to keep you waiting. We confused the entrances. We shall have to travel a little distance on the Metro, but not too far.' His English was excellent and there was only the slightest trace of his first language, Dutch. Later I discovered that his slight Dutch accent became more pronounced when he was tired.

We set off together to the entrance for the Moscow Metro, just a couple of hundred yards from the hotel. The Metro was busy with Russians glad to escape the stifling heat into the cool of its vast, ornate chambers. We caught a train and remained standing for the short journey to the Moscow suburb where George lived with his Russian wife, Ida. After twenty minutes or so, we emerged on to a busy suburban street.

'I hope you don't mind, but it is another short walk,' George said, somewhat apologetically.

I said that I didn't mind whatsoever and our route took us through what was clearly not a poor area of the city.

'We've recently moved to this district,' he said. 'There is the local Orthodox church. Would you like to look inside?'

I said that I would and I stepped into what was a fairly new and not particularly interesting building. As in many Moscow churches these days, there were many people praying before the icons. After a few moments, we went out again into the blazing sun and continued our walk, eventually arriving at the corner shop, where George stopped.

'My wife is at the dacha,' he said, 'so I need to get one or two items for our lunch.'

He bought some ham, cheese and salad, then we resumed our trek along the road, where there were two or three modern apartment blocks.

'It's a distance to the main entrance,' he said, as we approached one of the buildings. 'Do you mind if I take a short cut?'

I assured him that I didn't and he led the way. We came to some railings that were protecting the building. He stepped forward and gave one a gentle pull. It moved slightly and he squeezed through. I followed him.

'Old habits die hard, George,' I said, remembering how he had escaped from Wormwood Scrubs, where he served just over six years of his sentence, by squeezing through a prison window, the bars of which had been loosened. He smiled. We walked silently across the parched grass towards his apartment, to be greeted by the sound of hammering.

'They're making some improvements,' he said, as we entered the small lobby and climbed the stairs. 'Fortunately, at this time of the year we are at the dacha and don't have to suffer from the noise.

'This apartment is not as large as the one we moved from,' he remarked as we entered his flat. It was tastefully furnished and I imagined it was quite large by Moscow standards. Several oriental rugs covered the floor, and a colourful blanket was thrown over a settee. Scattered around the room were various silver trinkets of the type seen in many a souvenir shop across the Middle East. He went into the kitchen to prepare some coffee and I cast my eye across the bookcase well filled with English books. One caught my eye immediately: *British Foreign Policy: The years since Suez, 1956–1968*, written by the defector Donald Maclean. I took it down and noted that it was a proof copy, liberally marked with Maclean's annotations.

'Donald left me his library when he died,' Blake said as he put the coffee tray on to a low table. 'Do sit down, please.'

I sat opposite him and we sipped our coffee as someone in the next-door apartment hammered away.

'He is a retired general,' George said. 'He's been making alterations for weeks now and I'm afraid there is not much I can do about it.'

An hour or so before, when we first met outside the Rossiya, my first impression of Blake was how smart and well dressed he was. As we conversed, I now discovered that he was also naturally polite and courteous. It was difficult not to like him. He told me that he had agreed to meet with me because he was sure that I would not use anything I wrote about him for sensational purposes, and I assured him that this was so.

'My life has fallen in pleasant places,' he began, 'because I have been very, very lucky in every respect – probably more than many people would say that I deserve,' he began in reply to my asking him about his present way of life. 'I have this flat, which you see is very comfortable. In summer I am mostly in my dacha, which you will see tomorrow. I have a wife and have been happily married for thirty-two years. I still do a certain amount of work for the Institute of World Economy and International Relations, but I am not very hard pressed and am master of my own time. I have a car, but I don't use it very often. It's an old car by English standards. It's twelve years old, but it still runs very well.' He picked up a small photograph from the table and handed it to me. 'This is my grandson, who is beginning school in September and of whom we are very fond. He gives us a great deal of pleasure.'

By all accounts, George Blake had been a good family man. During the time he was working as a double agent in the UK, he was married with three small children. His wife at the time was the daughter of a senior military intelligence officer and it's not difficult to imagine his reaction when it was revealed that his son-in-law was working for the Russians. When Blake was given a forty-two-year sentence, his wife continued to visit him and also wrote to him regularly. George's mother maintained a good relationship with his wife who, as he admitted, was left in a very difficult position, similar to that of a widow with three young children to care for. After about six years, his wife visited him in prison and told him she had met a man who wanted to marry her, and asked if George would agree to a divorce.

'Of course,' said George, 'I could not refuse under the circumstances. What I could not tell her was that I was planning my escape. I couldn't be sure that I was going to succeed, but I hoped that if I reached safety, and I wasn't sure where I would find safety at that particular point, then she could join me and we could continue our life together. We had been very happy. The last year of our life together had been especially happy, when we were in the language school in southern Lebanon. I wasn't looking forward to going to court for the divorce case, but I escaped before that and unfortunately she was left high and dry, because I had disappeared. However, the authorities went a long way to meet her and arranged for her to be divorced in my absence, which I thought was quite right.'

Before visiting Moscow, I had read George Blake's book, *No Other Choice*, written many years earlier. I told him that when reading the book I had got the impression that the way he had deceived his wife hurt him.

'Yes, of course, very much,' he said immediately. 'My greatest feeling of guilt is towards her and the children, and also my mother and my sister, because they were the people who actually suffered. Of course you may say that the state suffered, but the state is an abstract notion.'

I didn't interrupt him at this point, but I supposed to myself that he was glossing over the fact that his deception may have cost the lives of many people. I determined to ask him about this later.

'My wife came from a conservative background; her father was a colonel in the Security Service and my activities came as a terrible shock to her. However, she was a brave woman and my mother was a very brave woman, and they helped each other and got through the crisis.'

He paused for a moment as he relived painful memories from the past.

'The first year here in Russia was very difficult for me, very difficult. I had hoped that perhaps when she knew I was here she would agree to come and join me. I knew of course that Melinda Maclean, who was an

American, had managed to come, to escape in a way. She came to join her husband and I felt disappointed that my wife had not done the same. Later, I got to know Maclean, first Philby and then Maclean, whom I got to know very well and I became friends with him and his wife and children. It was then I realized what a great blessing it was that my wife had never come here.'

'Why was that?' I asked.

'She could never have adapted to this kind of life, especially as it was lived then. I saw how difficult it was for Melinda Maclean and her children. The boy was nine when he came here and the younger one seven, and they never completely adapted, although they spoke fluent Russian and married Russian wives later. Maclean was also in a difficult position, because he felt guilt towards them. My wife was particularly English. Let me give you a small example. I remember we were living in Berlin in the mid-fifties and you could get everything in Berlin at that time as the shortages of the post-war period had disappeared. She would never buy anything for the children in the Berlin shops. She would always wait until she got back to England and buy things there. Only English things were acceptable. There is another reason. In Beirut I became great friends with another member on the language course. When I arrived in Moscow, he was also here as Minister at the British Embassy. His wife and my wife were also very good friends, and of course it would have been totally impossible for them to have had any communication. Given that, and all the shortages and difficult way of living, well, I began to realize that it was really a great blessing she did not come with me.

'The last time I saw her was about a month or six weeks before I escaped. When she remarried, and had another son by her second husband, she felt it wrong to continue to communicate directly with me and so we communicated through my mother, who would send me photographs of my children. My wife never said anything bad about me to the children. Whatever her feelings may have been, she never said anything derogatory, and my mother also spoke in favourable terms about me. However, there was no question of them coming with their mother to see me. Many years later, my middle son was in the Life Guards and served in Germany. When he was demobbed and free, as it were, he then said that he wanted to meet his father, and my mother arranged it. My wife did not object. I don't think she liked it very much, but she did not object. My wife's second husband, who died a few years ago, was a very good man and although he had a son of his own, he did not in any way favour his own son above my children. They all knew who I was, of course.

'So, my son came with my mother and my sister to East Berlin and we went to a seaside resort, where we had two weeks in extremely pleasant conditions. We got on extremely well together. It was a gamble, but my son, who was twenty-four at the time, looked very much like Misha, my son by my Russian wife, who was then about twelve. They got on well together and when he went back to England he told his brothers about his meeting with me and they also wanted to come. Eventually they came by train to the White Russian Station and I met them. Misha came with me and I recognized them immediately. They recognized me, although Anthony was only four when I left and the other had not even been born. He was born a month after my trial. They came to my flat and that night we had a very long talk. We talked about everything. I explained my motives, and the extraordinary thing is that they were both what is called committed Christians. It was this, I think, which helped them understand. Not approve. Not agree. But understand. From then on our relations have always been very warm and they write to me. I have been extraordinarily lucky, because it was really a gamble, especially that first night when I told them how it all went. It did not spoil our relations.'

Throughout the whole of our conversation, it was clear to me that George was very fond of all his children, as he was of his first wife. I asked him about the first years in Russia. Was it not an unusually solitary experience, living apart from his family in a foreign country?

'Yes, of course it was,' he replied. 'It was solitude, I suppose, but I have never thought of it in that way as, at first, I didn't actually live alone but with the man who helped me escape, Sean Bourke.'

Bourke was a member of the Committee of 100. He was a colourful character, to put it mildly. Following the escape, he too went to Moscow and shared a flat with George for a while. Their relationship deteriorated and eventually, after being totally unable to settle to life in the Soviet Union, Bourke returned to the UK, where he died prematurely in his forties.

'Yes, it was solitude, because I had not adapted, and although Bourke and I lived in a flat together, we were very different people. A man from the service, the KGB, came to visit regularly, but we were by ourselves and we did not know anybody, nor did we have contact with anyone. We had enough money, but we could not spend it, as in Moscow in those days there was very little to spend it on. There were restaurants, but they were not very nice. There were no night clubs or bars or anything of that kind, so we lived a very isolated existence. Then my mother came out and we went on holiday to the Carpathian Mountains, which was very nice. Then she went back to Holland in the summer, but just before my birthday in November, she returned with my things and started to live with me. Sean Bourke moved out into another flat of his own and my mother stayed with me for almost a year.'

According to George, his mother made herself quite at home in Moscow. It was unusual for foreigners to buy things in ordinary Russian shops, as there were special shops for their use, but his mother overcame all the difficulties and made no small impression on the local shopkeepers.

Once again, I returned to the question of how he coped with his unusual way of life. He stood, took a sweet from a small bowl, and sat down again.

'From the very beginning, as a small boy, I have always been somebody apart; not alone, but apart. Now why has that been? I will show you a photograph and you will see at once that this is my father, who was a Spanish Jew from Turkey. He served in the British Army and was in charge of a British Army unit in Holland after the First World War. This unit arranged the transfer of British prisoners of war from Germany to England. Now this is my father.'

He passed me a framed photograph and pointed to a man of dark complexion in British Army uniform standing next to a fair-haired lady.

'And this is my mother. As you can see, they are very different persons. What I mean is that from the very beginning I lived in Holland with my Dutch family who were different from me. My sisters were big with a fair complexion – well, they were Dutch. I was also Dutch, of course. I spoke Dutch and went to a Dutch school, but there was something . . . I was not like the others. I was dark and small and so I stood out and looked different from my mother, so that set me apart a bit. Even my uncles and aunts looked on me as something a little special. Not in a negative sense. On the contrary, they were very fond of me and I was a favourite grandson of my grandmother, partly because I was different from the ordinary run of her grandchildren. And so this has run through all my life. All the time, wherever I have been, I have been apart, but also a little bit different. I have the same now. I am integrated into this society completely and I get on very well and feel quite at home. But I know, and they know, I am not quite like them.

'It is a very small thing, but the other week my small grandson said to me, "I am Russian, but you are not." I said, "Well, I know. I congratulate you!" He knows that I am not like his father or his mother or his grandparents and that has been part of my life always. In England I was in the Secret Service. I was in the Navy. I was in Cambridge. In all these traditional English institutions I was accepted, but at the same time I knew I was not. I was not quite part of it and they also knew it, although they did not show it. I think that is the element of solitude I have experienced.'

We sat silently for a moment. The hammering in the flat next door had ceased and it was quiet.

'Was there ever a point in your life when you felt that you belonged?' I asked.

'No, I don't think so.'

'What about your immediate family now?'

He paused before he spoke. 'Well . . . of course in my family I belong, but the story of my little grandson is his view of me, not mine of him, but it is typical. My wife and I have an excellent relationship and I love my son and he loves me, and I am very fortunate that I am very fond of my daughter-in-law, really very fond of her and she of me. But that is a different thing. It does not mean that they don't feel I am different, you see.

'My wife knows that I am not Russian. If I had been a Russian maybe she would have treated me differently. I don't know. It is difficult to say, but throughout my life there has always been this element of being different. Maybe the fact that you know you don't quite belong is, in itself, a source of solitude.'

Again we remained silent as I pondered the strangeness of his existence. Here, speaking with me, was a man who had always felt apart. Even now, established in Russia for many years and surrounded by his family, he continued to feel that he was different.

'Did the fact that you had always had such feelings influence your choice of career?' I asked.

'Do you mean my choice of career as an intelligence officer or as a Russian spy?'

'Both.'

'Well, as an intelligence officer that was just a sort of normal progression. When I lived in occupied Holland I joined the Underground as a very young man. I looked even younger than I actually was. I was a courier and carried messages from one group to another. Eventually I escaped to England, through France and Spain, because I wanted to become an agent and wanted to be sent back to Holland as a British agent to work with an Underground group. I wanted to control an Underground group and receive my instructions from London. Of course, if you want to join the Secret Service they never accept you, but I tried, even though I did not know where to start. Anyway, I joined the Navy and got a commission after a course in the RNVR [Royal Naval Volunteer Reserve]. On the last day of the course, just before we were promoted, a man came round from the Admiralty and listed all the ships we could serve on, from battleships to cruisers to submarines to speedboats. He said that we could choose, but there was no guarantee that we would get what we chose. At the end of the list he said that there were special services, but he didn't know what it all meant. All he knew was that people disappeared and then later reappeared. When he said that, I said to myself, *This is what I want. This is being an agent if he cannot say why people disappear and reappear.* So, very recklessly, I put my name down and we were then sent home on leave for a week.

'I had been at home for a week when I got a letter from the Admiralty saying that I had to report to submarine headquarters in Portsmouth. I thought, *Submarines? I'm not very interested in submarines,* but I still went there. When I arrived, it turned out they were one- or two-man submarines and as I had put my name down I could not get out of it. The training was extremely dull because I had to spend three or four hours at the bottom of Portsmouth Harbour in a diving suit, followed by a visit to some place in Scotland. We had to undergo a test of diving to a considerable depth. I lost consciousness and was not eligible to go for further training, so they found me a job as Officer of the Watch until they could find another appointment for me.

'The commander, whose name was also Blake, took a liking to me. I don't know what he did behind the scenes, but he told me to go to London for an interview. I went to a house in Parliament Street, where I was interviewed by a naval captain. I thought it was all part of the Navy. I had to write out my autobiography and tell him my story, after which I was sent back to Portsmouth. A few days later, I was called back to London to see a number of other people. I was still thinking it was the Navy, as there was talk about speedboats. The Secret Service had a special flotilla of speedboats used to drop agents on the Continent, but the word "secret" was never mentioned.'

The telephone rang and George went into the other room to answer it. In a few moments he returned.

'That was my son Misha. He will bring us back from the dacha tomorrow. Now, what was I saying? Ah yes, once again I was called to this house in London and there I was taken to see a colonel in the Marines. I was still under the impression that it was something to do with the Admiralty, until he told me very solemnly that I had been accepted for work in the Secret Service. I was absolutely elated. I could not believe it. It was then that I was sent to work in the Dutch section of the service.' He paused once more as I pondered my next question.

'As you look back on those years,' I asked, 'are you able to understand your motives for wanting to belong to the Secret Service? Was it for reasons of patriotism, or were there different reasons?'

'That is not difficult to answer,' he said without hesitation. 'Ever since the start of the war, and especially the invasion of Holland and the bombing of Rotterdam, I had been filled with a great hatred for the Germans. And, of course, for what they were doing against the Jews. Although I was not brought up as a Jew at all, I was brought up as a Protestant by my mother, but still I knew that I was partly of Jewish descent. I saw how the Jews were being rounded up and so I was filled with great hatred for the Germans, and especially for the Nazis. I thought it was my duty, in fact my pleasure, to do anything to fight them and there was no problem there at the time. No problem at all.'

The DIY enthusiast resumed his banging on the wall as we continued our conversation. There had been much speculation over the years as to why George Blake, comfortably situated in the British Secret Service, had offered his services to the Russians. I wanted to hear from his own mouth the reasons he had for taking such a step.

'Why,' I asked, somewhat bluntly, 'did you become an agent for the Russians? Have you been able to look back and see what caused you to change?'

He answered immediately. 'Oh yes. It was a question of stages, of course, but I should go back a bit into the history of my early life and my family. As I told you, my father came from a wealthy Jewish family in Constantinople. Those people loved everything that was French, although my father was a naturalized British subject. His name was Albert Behar.'

'How did you get the name of Blake?' I asked.

'Well, my mother was a British subject by marriage and she was told that she could leave for England on one of the last destroyers from Holland. She did so and went first of all to a refugee camp, as she had no relations whatsoever in England. She made friends with a lady who was quite well off and lived in Hampstead, and eventually she went to live with this family. The lady had an elderly mother who lived in Chalfont St Peter, in a cottage there. My mother had a very attractive personality and went to take care of the elderly lady, while my sisters worked in a local hospital. The name of the lady was Blake and she thought it best for my mother to take an English name. My mother agreed and the name of Blake was chosen. That is how it happened.'

He continued his narrative. 'The Cairo family loved French civilization and they spoke French. They were called Sephardic Jews. My father's next of kin in Egypt and other parts of the Middle East and Turkey were very wealthy. He died when I was thirteen and he left my mother in very difficult financial circumstances. My father met her immediately after the war, when he was an officer in the British Army, so that was how she saw him. He never told her that he was Jewish. My grandmother, who lost her husband in the Spanish flu epidemic of nineteen eighteen, let my father come to the house because one of her brothers wanted to practise his English. That, and being a soldier all alone, led my grandmother to give her permission. Of course, there were attractive young women at home – my mother was one of them. They fell in love, but my grandmother did not like that at all. She did not want my mother to marry a foreigner; she wanted her to marry a Dutchman. She did not know he was Jewish, although she could have known by looking at him, but people were not so cosmopolitan in those days. He had a British uniform and so that sort of confirmed it all. In the end they eloped, went to England and got married in London. Obviously my grandmother was furious, but eventually they returned to Holland.'

As George related his family history, I realized that there had been concealment from the beginning. His father did not tell his mother that he was Jewish. In fact, according to George, he told her very little about his background. He did not take her to his family, who were then living in France, because they would not have appreciated the fact that he had married a Gentile. So he set up a business in Holland, but he was not a good businessman. He was also plagued with ill health due to having been gassed during the war. They had children and were very happy together, but life was difficult, especially as George's father did not speak Dutch and did not want to learn it.

'I suppose you could say that my father had oriental views. He did not listen to the advice of his wife and she could have given him very good advice on how to behave with the Dutch people. However, he did not listen, and then came the crisis in nineteen twenty-nine, his business failed and he got lung cancer. He died at the age of forty-three, which was in nineteen thirty-three. I think, leaving my mother with considerable debts.' George remained silent for a moment as his mind went back across the years.

'Before he died, he said to my mother that if she needed help she should turn to his sister, the wife of a rich banker in Cairo. My mother's family was a middle-class family of civil servants, officers and ministers of the Church, but they could not help my mother.'

'Was this when you went to live in Cairo?' I asked.

'A friend of ours went to Cairo on business and he visited my father's sister, who promised to help. She didn't want to send money to a woman she didn't know, but she said that the oldest boy [the only boy, in fact] could be sent over and he would be given a good education and set up for life.'

George's mother had been very much in two minds as to whether he ought to go to Cairo. She left the choice to him. Although he was very attached to his Dutch family, a sense of adventure was a part of his make-up, so he decided to go. In Egypt he found himself living in a palatial house, complete with servants. In the summer the family travelled throughout Europe, and George was told he was welcome to accompany them. Instead he went to Holland to see his mother.

As French was spoken in the Cairo family, and he only spoke Dutch, they sent him to a French *lycée*. At first they wanted to send him to a Jesuit school, where his cousins had been pupils, but as he had been brought up a Protestant, the thought horrified him, so it was to the *lycée* he went. Then, after the first year, because his father had acquired British citizenship, he was sent to the English school in Cairo, where he learned the language and got an English education.

It was at this point in our conversation that George gave another insight into what may have caused him to take such a momentous decision years later.

'The main thing I have not touched upon yet is that I had two cousins who were older than I was. You may have heard of one of them: Henri Curiel. Have you heard of him?'

I said that I was familiar with the name but knew very little about him.

'He was a . . .' George hesitated for a moment. 'Well,' he continued, 'he upheld the causes of the Third World. He was murdered in Paris in nineteen seventy-nine [in fact it was 1978]. He was eight years older than I and as a young man very attractive and very well spoken. He had decidedly communist views and later became one of the founders of the Communist Party in Egypt. Of course, he lived in the same house as I did and we became good friends. He used to take me out to his father's farms. His father had many. He felt a feeling of guilt for the fate of the Egyptian fellas who were terribly poor. Every weekend he would distribute medicine and eye drops, and there were times when I would go with him. He began to realize that distributing eye drops and medicine was not good enough and that the whole system had to be changed, so he became a convinced communist, along with his elder brother. It was the time of the Spanish Civil War and we talked a great deal about this. There was one thing which stopped me from agreeing with him completely and that was that I was a very religious boy. I used to go to church twice on Sunday and the fact was that in communist countries, and especially in Spain at that time, the Church was persecuted, and monks and priests and nuns were murdered in Russia. That was something I could not accept. I now realize that many of the things he said to me were a source of one of the motives which made me change my views. Later on I ceased being a Christian in the strict sense of that word. In theory I hoped that communism would wipe out all social distinctions. But it did not work out like that. The Krogers [former Soviet spies who operated in the UK for many years before being detected] attached no importance at all to what race or class you belonged to. That explains why, in the first instance, there were so many Jews who were communists. Like my cousins, for example. They saw a way out of the difficulty of being a Jew. One part of Jewry put their hope in Zionism. Another in the creation of the communist state.'

By now, the neighbour had increased his banging on the wall and it became more and more difficult to hear. We stumbled on for a few moments while George told me how, during the war, he had developed a great admiration for the Soviet effort in fighting the Germans. Eventually he was sent to Downing College, Cambridge, to learn Russian under the tutorship of the legendary Elizabeth Hill.

'The idea was,' he said, 'that you should know your enemies. I was the only Secret Service officer on the course. The others were from different branches of the military. I took the course very seriously but soon realized that I could not work properly in Cambridge itself due to the many diversions, so I decided to move away from the town and board with a vicar's wife, who took me in on reasonable terms.'

The noise of banging had now become so disruptive that we decided to move to another room, where it was a little quieter. It was suggested that we ought to take a break for lunch, so we moved once again into the kitchen, where George prepared a light meal which we ate together seated around the kitchen table. I had to admit to myself that George Blake was a very likeable man and a complex one to boot.

As we ate, he spoke of the other notorious defectors and double agents: Burgess, Maclean and Philby. He had known all three of them in Moscow, but Maclean was the only one of the trio he respected. They were thrown together and many petty disputes occurred between them. Philby had a major falling out with Blake over a seemingly ludicrous matter. Blake had been awarded the Order of Lenin and, at the time, Philby remained undecorated. This led to a major break in relationships between the two men. Later Philby received the same award. That small event indicated to me how strained life had become in the strange secluded world of the defector, although similar jealousies continue to this day within the ranks of the British Civil Service and, I imagine, within most bureaucracies.

After lunch George continued his narrative.

'I became one of the favourite pupils of Elizabeth Hill. She was the daughter of an English merchant in St Petersburg and she looked typically Russian. She hated communism but was a great Russian patriot. She was a very devout Orthodox and some of her favourite pupils used to go with her to the Russian church in London. She taught us history and literature, and she inspired in me a great interest in Russia and an affection for things Russian. The funny thing is that I have lived for thirty years in Russia and I know the reality very well, but I have not lost my romantic feelings for Russia. This feeling about Russia was another step in my development. I did not regard them as the people without a soul, and I began to have a great liking and respect for them, although I had not been to Russia.

'At the same time there came this change in my religious views. If God was omnipotent, then I could not see the necessity for a redeemer, and the role of Christ was not really necessary. When I was sent to Korea I continued to attend church, partly because it was my habit but also because I hoped that, through contact with the missionaries, I could find Koreans whom I might recruit to the Intelligence Service. I became great friends with the bishop and especially with the vicar, Father Hunt, who was a very nice man and Commissioner Lord of the Salvation Army.

My main intelligence task was to penetrate the Maritime Provinces, Vladivostok, but I soon realized that there was no contact whatsoever between the Provinces and Korea. We had been given instructions to stay put when war broke out, with the hope that we might become an observation point for as long as we were tolerated, so we had no doubt that we would stay. I was Head of Station, a very small station.

'With hindsight it was stupid to stay, as we had no means of communication and we did not have our own wireless station. So one of the first things that happened was that Cable & Wireless closed down. It all happened very quickly. We stayed, but we advised most of the British community to leave. The French were in the same position as we were. They too had been given instructions to stay. The city [Seoul] had been occupied by the North, and there was fighting, so many of the religious personnel came and stayed with us. For the first few days we lived peacefully. There was a Union Jack flying high up on the minister's house. A Korean major came and told us to haul it down, as it might affect aircraft. I had a very bad impression of the Korean government. I knew they used torture, and one of their ministers was a great admirer of Hitler. He had a picture of him in his room. University professors, who in the UK would be considered mildly Labour, were considered communist. I formed a very unfavourable picture of South Korea and a more favourable picture of North Korea, although I didn't know a great deal about it. In relation to this I want to say that I have always been anti-American. Not that I don't like Americans, there are many Americans I like, but I don't like the manifestation of American civilization.'

The picture George was painting for me was that of a gradual drift towards communism going way back to his childhood friendship with Henri Curiel. I recollected that he had told me in a casual conversation that he did not like situations in which opposition was stifled. I put it to him that he had come to Moscow over thirty years ago when there was no opposition to the regime. How did he relate to that? He admitted that it caused him problems.

'I found that to be the difficult side of the communist regime, but I found an explanation for it. I remember talking to Peter Kroger about it, as he also felt it to be a difficulty. He had been an American in opposition to the American government. How does one build a communist society if there is a constant possibility of being removed by the ballot box? What you had started would all be brought to nothing and you would have to start again. It wasn't possible to build a communist society in that way.

Donald Maclean thought it would be wonderful if there was a communist society which tolerated opposition.

'There was one other thing we all found very difficult to stomach and that was that people were not allowed to travel freely. To travel, you had to be accepted in a tourist group, and to be accepted was extremely difficult. Before that you had to see a psychiatrist to confirm that you were not mad. You also could not go with your wife or your children. Someone always had to be left behind. This was one of the darkest sides of life. One of the excuses was that there was not enough hard currency. That was partly true, but I don't think it was the main reason. They were afraid of any foreign influence. However, although there was no opposition that could manifest itself, there was opposition that expressed itself in discussions in the kitchen, when friends met to say what they really thought. I am not talking about the dissidents. They were the courageous people who came out openly. They tried to, anyway. By the time I came to the Soviet Union, the majority of the people no longer believed in communism. Up to Stalin's time they did. The Second World War, or the Great Patriotic War as they called it here, gave a boost to the system which had been successful in defending the country against the foreign invader, but it was more nationalistic than communist. In the end, it was that strong inner opposition that caused the system to break down. The people no longer believed in it.'

'Did it come as a surprise to you when you came here?'

He was quick and frank with his answer. 'Yes, it came as a surprise to me. Many manifestations came as a surprise. I was rather naive, I suppose.'

'Was it a disappointment?'

'Well, of course – a great disappointment. It wasn't so much the material conditions – whether there were ten kinds of sausage or thirty kinds of cheese – but the fact that I began to realize that no new man was born here, which was supposed to happen. The ideal of Lenin was that you did away with private property and everything would belong to the state. People as a result would very quickly change their attitude to private property and would see the benefit of public property and help each other and become in many ways new people. A little bit like born-again Christians in a way. But it didn't happen, at least in the space that history allotted to communism, and there were no signs it was happening.'

'Could it be,' I asked, 'that having rejected spiritual regeneration through Christ you looked for it in political terms and didn't find it there either?'

'Yes. I think that is a very good way of putting it, yes.' He continued with his previous train of thought. 'I can't say there was no opposition. There was. That opposition in the end was the deciding factor. It wasn't American arms or American pressure. What caused the downfall of the system was that people no longer believed in it. People hadn't changed. You can't build a perfect system with imperfect people. So, communism could not be brought about and there was this inner opposition to it. There was this enormous gap between the official propaganda and the reality that everybody knew. But, if I may go back a moment. A man like Donald Maclean, who was a very convinced communist, believed that the old regime would eventually die out and be replaced by technocrats who would give communism a human face. He didn't see that. He died before Perestroika. When they tried seriously to change the system and improve things, it collapsed. It was so rigid. If you took away one small stone the next would fall, and in the end the whole system crumbled.'

I began to ask him a question about Donald Maclean, for whom he had very great admiration, but he interrupted me and went to get a photograph.

'Let me show you what a fine face he had,' said George.

I took the photograph and noted that indeed Maclean had been a handsome man. 'Clearly he was a very different character from Philby,' I said.

'Philby and Maclean were convinced communists. I am not in any way questioning Philby's sincerity. But he was a man who liked adventure and he was a man who was attracted by the business of spying. He enjoyed outwitting other people. He got a certain kick out of it. Of that I am quite sure. Now, Maclean was quite the opposite. He didn't like spying. He didn't like deceiving people. He felt that it was his duty. He was placed in life in such a way that he could make a real contribution to the cause, and he couldn't refuse it. That was a big sacrifice he made in his life. The other was giving up his ambition to become a university don. That was his ambition. In the early days his controller had told him that he must leave the Communist Party and leave his roots and get into the Foreign Office. He did that, to the great relief of his mother. He became a Foreign Office official, which actually he didn't like at all. He didn't like the social side of life, but he felt it was necessary and he made his sacrifice.'

Returning to the question of solitude, I said that there was certainly a solitary aspect to the life of a spy who constantly had to conceal matters, even from his own family. I suggested that this might be especially so for a double agent.

'Yes, I suppose it is. Yes,' replied George.

'How did you face and deal with that?' I asked.

'Well, I behaved – at least I tried to behave, and I think I succeeded – as I would have behaved anyway. I behaved towards my colleagues as if I wasn't committed to the communist cause. I also learned one thing, and that is that people are not really interested in your views. So, except for the Suez crisis when I did make my views known, I tended to keep quiet and so I never had to lie.'

In George Blake's book, *No Other Choice*, he says that there was no important document that crossed his desk in the ten years he was in his post in London that he did not pass to the Russians. I asked him if this was correct and he said it was. I then asked him if he felt that one day he might be discovered. His answer surprised me.

'I realized that the chances of not being discovered were very small,' he began. 'On the other hand, one keeps on, in a position like that, hoping for the best. I always hoped that nothing would happen. The danger was in my regular meetings with my Soviet counterpart. I had very great confidence in him, and when I went to a meeting I was sure that I wasn't being followed. I also knew that as long as I wasn't suspected I wouldn't be followed. There was one thing I could not do anything about and that was if someone, such as a defector, gave me away and, of course, that is exactly what happened. In one way I am grateful that I was discovered then, because if I had continued, now that Perestroika has come about I would certainly have been uncovered and I would have lived under constant fear of being discovered.'

'Were there times in those ten years when you were almost exposed?'

'No, not that I know of at all. No one suspected me. I know that. My former colleagues told me that at first, when the suspicion came round to me, they didn't want to believe it. There is one other interesting point in this connection. I repeatedly asked my opposite number, who, as I said, was a very skilled operator, what my attitude should be if I was arrested and questioned. He said, "I don't want to talk about that. If we start talking about that you are already halfway to being discovered. You must put this out of your mind completely."

'Is he still around?' I asked.

'No. He was in his middle fifties when I was in my thirties. He died a few months after I arrived in Moscow. I met him over here but he died shortly afterwards.'

'Was it a relief to you when you were discovered?'

'Well, that is an interesting question. It was. Before you are discovered you are continually living with the fear that you might be discovered. Although you learn to live with this, once you have been discovered, then obviously that fear disappears. The people who discovered you and arrested you then become afraid that you might run away from them. So the fear is transferred from one side to the other.'

'We have got slightly ahead of ourselves in the story,' I said. 'Can we go back a bit? I'm interested to know the point at which you made the decision to change.'

'Change what?' he asked.

'To go to the other side.'

'Oh yes, I remember, that was during the Korean War. But gradual changes had already taken place and the war acted as a catalyst.'

'So, when you came back to the UK after the Korean War you were already committed?'

'I was committed, yes.'

We both remained silent again. Then I enquired: 'When you returned home you were working alongside colleagues, some of whom were friends.'

He understood my question before I had put it to him clearly.

'Yes, I know. That is very difficult, but I think I can answer it. Maybe it is a kind of self-deception of drawing a very sharp dividing line between the personal and the official. I worked with people I liked and some I did not like. Just as in any office. I did not consider that what I was doing was directed against them personally. It was not even directed against Britain, because I am a great admirer of Britain and the British people. I admire their qualities, which I especially appreciated during the years of the war, when I was in England, and also when I lived very closely with them as a prisoner in Wormwood Scrubs. My actions were not directed against them personally. It was simply that I thought a communist system would be more just and equitable and a better way of life for humanity than the capitalist system with its profit-making motives. I still believe that, despite everything that has happened. I believe it is unattainable at the moment, because ordinary people here in Russia, and in England, in fact anywhere, are not ready for that. They are not ready because if you want to build a communist society everybody must put the interests of their neighbours, of their friends and of their community above their own personal interests. That is the same with Christianity. It has not been possible to build a Christian society in the true sense of the word.

I believe it is possible for people to change and, in time, people will move towards that society, but never by force. Let me return to the question of deception. My family has always been closer to me than anything else.'

'Would it be true to say that the deception against your family affected you more than the deception against your colleagues?'

His answer was now less precise.

'Well, in the first place, yes. You can put things in categories. With my family it was more intense. Why? Because I knew they would suffer. My colleagues would not suffer, or were unlikely to suffer. Of course, a lot goes on in one's mind at the time and one just pushes it out. I didn't think too much about what might happen if things went wrong. If you do, then of course you are lost. You must not do that. But let's get back to the feeling of deception. My actions were not directed against my family, nor was I acting against the British people, although I suppose I was in a way. It all depends on how you look at it. I felt at the time that the British people would benefit from a communist society if it came about.'

'But it is said that you named names. In other words, you turned people in.'

'That is not true at all. No one has been mentioned who has suffered as a result of my work, and when I was tried, as you may well know, there was nothing in the indictment that mentioned agents of any sort. It was a ridiculous story put about by George Brown [former British Foreign Secretary] that I had been given forty-two years because there were forty-two agents who had died. That is ridiculous. It would mean the British government assesses the life of an agent to be worth one year, wouldn't it?'

I didn't respond to his rhetorical question, but thought to myself that it would never be known if, or how many, people suffered as a result of his actions. If he was passing critical information to the Russians for much of the time he was working for the British Intelligence Service it might be reasonable to conclude that some people suffered in one way or another. We shall never know, as the exact consequences of his actions are probably impossible to determine with any degree of accuracy.

At this point we changed tack again and I asked him if, with reference to an earlier point he had made, he believed that men and women would ever be ready for the type of society that was enshrined within his under-standing of communism.

'I shall tell you my views on that and also the reason why I ceased to be a Christian in the strict sense of the word. I don't believe any more that Christ is the Son of God and that he died to redeem sinners. I don't believe that and I will tell you why. I was brought up as a Calvinist and believe in predestination to this day. I believe that everything that happens in this world, and in our personal lives, is ordained by God and that we are part of his plan; whether we do good or bad, we are part of his plan. We must do it. Although we may think we are free – we have the illusion of being free – we cannot act at any time differently from how we act and therefore I believe that God is the author of what we humans call good and evil, but it is only good and evil to us. God has got quite different ideas and quite different plans. It is very simple. Two countries go to war. Both have prayed to God for a victory. One gets the victory and the other does not. Well, that is because God wants it like that, not because one country is better than another.'

'Are you evading personal responsibility for your actions by believing in what you have just said?'

'That is true, but it also has the other side to it. I don't feel that when I am praised for anything that I deserve the praise. I am not responsible really for the bad things I do, so I am not responsible for the good things I do.'

My next question was inevitable. 'So,' I asked, 'what are you responsible for?'

'I am just an instrument in the hands of God. That is how I see it.'

So this is how he justifies his life, I thought. *This is how he lives with the fact that for much of his adult life he worked for the establishment of an ideal state brought about by communism and now the whole edifice has collapsed.*

I returned to my questioning again. 'If you say you are just an instrument, would you not say that such a concept considerably reduces humanity?'

'Well, that may be so, but I believe that God has a plan and that we are still developing. I don't know what that is – nobody knows and probably nobody will ever know until the end of time, you see. Life confirms to me that everything is preordained. We may be due to leave this flat at a certain moment, but then I say to you, "Have another cup of tea." That is something completely without moral implications. You say "Yes" and as a result we stay ten minutes longer. Then we find ourselves in the Metro just as a bomb goes off. Everything in life is interconnected. Anyone who believes in God accepts that life and death are in his hands. He ordains the time of the death and the circumstances of our birth. If I am born out of an act of adultery, then it was God who created that situation. If I am killed by the hand of a murderer, it was God who created that also. That is how I see it.'

I was interested to hear how he related this strict interpretation of predestination to his former belief in communism, so I asked whether in the past, when he followed communist teaching, he abandoned his belief in God.

'No, I did not,' he said emphatically.

'How, then,' I queried, 'did you reconcile the concept of predestination and lack of free will with your belief as a communist?'

His answer was simple. 'Because I believed that that also was a part of God's plan. I believe that everything that happens is part of God's plan.'

'But the concept of God was inconsistent with belief in communism and a Marxist concept.'

'Not really. It was the anti-Church movement within communism. Before the revolution, the not very Christian behaviour of the Orthodox Church made this so. The Church was supported entirely by the Tsarist autocracy.'

By this time, George had made his views clear. I told him that I could not subscribe to them and further said that by believing what he did he seemed to have reverted to his childhood and resigned himself to what he regarded as the inevitable. One might say that he had come full circle.

'Yes,' he said, 'I think there is a lot in what you say.'

'Is this the way you have resolved the problem of your identity?' I asked.

'Maybe,' he replied, 'maybe. My position may be wrong, but I find the concept of God and human free will completely irreconcilable.'

'Let me ask you a question you may find difficult to answer,' I said, as we drew towards the end of our brief theological conversation. 'If you had your time over again, say from the time of Korea . . .'

Before I could finish, he interrupted me. 'I know the question. I find the answer very difficult to give, because I don't know what would have happened.'

'Do you have regrets?'

'No, I don't think there are regrets. As I said, and I repeat again, my only regret is a feeling of guilt that I have towards my family. There is no regret as far as I can say about whether my life would have been much better if I had done this or that. If I had not done this, would my life have been better? Would I have been a better man? Would I have been happier whatever value one attaches to life? Would those values have been satisfied more than they are now? Then my answer is no because I have had a very interesting life and have met very many unusual people. I have met people I consider saints – saints even in the Christian sense of the word. Yes, I have had some very unusual experiences.'

I was fascinated to hear from him who were the saints to which he referred, so I asked him the question.

'Well, for instance, I regard Donald Maclean as a saint, because he was a man who was completely detached from all personal interest. He lived soberly. He was not interested at all in position or money, or in rewards. He lived very simply according to his own views of what is right. He was very hard-working and a very good father to his family. He suffered for them because of the position he had put them in. He was very kind to people and had no sense of superiority. He was also very modest and so I think that he had all the qualities of a saint and he sacrificed himself to the cause that he believed in. The other people I knew very well and was also very fond of and admired greatly were the Krogers – Helen and Peter. They were people of the same kind: very modest and very simple and also very brave, with a great gift for friendship and a great interest in other people. I regard them too as very saintly people. Then in Korea I used to know a Monsignor MacQuill, who was a parish priest, and he was with us in the internment camp. He was a very jolly Irishman and was always helping people and keeping up their spirits. He was a big man, like yourself, and he was not afraid. He was very brave and a man I admired very greatly. I considered him as a saintly person who was an example to me.'

I couldn't help but think to myself that that was the best write-up Donald Maclean and the Krogers had had for some time. I resumed my questioning.

'Is it important to you what others think of you?'

He answered without hesitation. 'No. I have been hardened.'

'Where were you hardened?'

'Well, my experience after conviction. So many unpleasant things have been said about me, but I don't react to them very strongly. But I must tell you this. There is a saying of St Paul that some vessels are made to honour and some to dishonour. I am in the extraordinary position of being a vessel which has been made both to honour and dishonour. In England I am in dishonour and I can understand that. It is perfectly right. Here in Russia I am in honour and that is a rather extraordinary position to be in. In my daily life, of course I experience more of the feeling of being a respected citizen, but I know very well what the people of England think of me.'

We had been talking for a long time, so I asked George if we might take a few moments for a break.

'Let's have a cup of tea,' he suggested.

He went into the kitchen to boil the water and I fiddled with my small recording machine, anxious to make sure that it had recorded our conversation adequately. George returned and continued immediately.

'I must tell you the story of my escape. It is quite extraordinary.'

That was an understatement. His escape from HMP Wormwood Scrubs stunned the nation, and to this day there are people who believe that he must have been assisted in this feat by British Intelligence, the KGB, or both!

'What struck me as remarkable,' I began, 'was that the person who went to break the bar on the window through which you escaped, just put his foot against it and it gave way, just like that! I know many British prisons, and I find that one fact remarkable.'

He nodded. 'You must understand that it was not the bar of my cell. It was the long narrow window at the end of the block. I too couldn't understand it. My fellow prisoner who went to break it was back so quickly that I thought something had gone wrong. "It was so rusty," he said to me, "all I had to do was give it one kick and it gave way."'

As I found this difficult to believe, I asked, 'That is true, is it?'

'Of course it is true,' he replied immediately.

'What was your reaction to the speculation there was about your escape?'

'The obvious thing was that the police and the SIS thought it was the KGB who had done it. The police and the Security Service felt from the beginning that they were up against an opponent who was very difficult to deal with. Of course, it wasn't the KGB at all. If they had known that, they may well have searched more diligently.'

I have to confess that to this day I find it hard to credit that a window in the prison could be in such poor condition that one kick alone would be sufficient to break the centre bar. However, that is the story George Blake sticks to and from which he does not deviate. From the very beginning of his sentence he was looking for ways in which he might escape. He did not believe that the KGB would help him as, so he said, they would not wish to run the risk of a major international scandal should something go wrong. So he began looking for people from both within the prison and on the outside who might assist him.

In early 1962 his chance came. In prison he met Michael Randle and Pat Pottle, who were both members of the Committee of 100 and each serving an eighteen-month sentence. They, along with Sean Bourke, were the ones he named who gave him assistance on the grounds that they believed forty-two years to be a totally inhuman sentence. To complete the story of the escape, which has been well documented elsewhere, a rope-type ladder was thrown over the wall, which he scaled. On the other side, he fell and broke his wrist, which was later tended by a sympathetic doctor. For some days he stayed in a flat near to the prison and then was concealed in a compartment of a camper van and driven to East Berlin.

'What was the reaction of the KGB when they learned you had escaped?' I asked.

'Well, they were just as surprised as MI6.'

'They could not understand it?'

'They could not understand it and they did not know any more about what had happened than the British did. All they did was to send telegrams to their various posts to warn them that I might turn up somewhere. That was all they could do. They did not know.'

'Did your Russian contact get in touch?' I queried.

'No,' was the definite answer.

I put it to him that, given the fact that he was an important person to the Russians, they might well have given him a plan to put into operation should he fall into difficulties. He assured me yet again that he was given no such plan.

'However,' he said, 'as soon as I arrived back in England from Beirut I was under constant observation.'

'Let me go back a bit, George,' I said, interested to learn more about his recall to London for questioning. 'When you were called back from the language school, you need not have gone. Did you not smell a rat, so to speak? Did you not think something was wrong?'

'I did, but I was not quite sure. It was nineteen sixty-one and the war was raging in the Congo, with the result that many government people were moving around. I thought that I might possibly be moved and, of course, I had previously been recalled. If I had known for sure, I would not have gone back – of course not. I might have gone to Damascus. Philby, you may remember, was put on a Soviet ship in Beirut harbour.'

What Blake did not know at the time was that a Polish defector had indicated that there were top-level leaks and British Intelligence had narrowed the suspects down to about five, Blake being one. A friend of mine, who at the time was a young officer in British Intelligence, told me that when George was recalled for questioning, no one could believe that he was in any way involved. 'What – George?' they said. 'Certainly not George.'

'When you were recalled and questioned, you virtually gave yourself away, didn't you?' I continued.

'Well, I didn't . . . It was not like that. I was questioned . . . What shall I say? They started a long way off and it was all done in a very friendly tone. They kept on getting closer and closer, and it came to the point – I think it must have been the end of the first day – when they more or less accused me of working for the Russians. I denied it. I was allowed to go home and I went to my mother's and stayed there. The next morning they sent a car and I returned to face more questioning. Finally they said, "Well, we know you have done it," and I denied it. And they said, "Well, if you did not, then it was somebody you knew who did it." The other person they mentioned was a very nice man and they tried to put me in the position where I had to say it was either him or me. I said that it was their business and I knew nothing about it. I went home again and the car returned the next morning and we continued the conversation. After lunch they went on a different tack. By the way, these were people I knew quite well. Then they said [with reference to his days in Korea], "We know that you did it, but we realize that it was not your fault and you could not help it if you were tortured and had to admit you were working for the secret police." They suggested that I had been blackmailed, and then something happened that I find very difficult to explain today.' He paused for a moment. 'I said that I was not tortured and nobody had blackmailed me. Nobody forced me. It was I myself who had offered my services and that was my true confession, and then they had it.'

He paused again and I imagined how his interrogators must have felt at that dramatic moment. As though he could read my thoughts he continued. 'They were never rude towards me. They never used force and were always very polite – one might say sympathetic. They did a great deal for my wife and they helped my mother. From what I know – I cannot be certain – there were two schools of thought in the SIS One wanted to give no publicity to the case at all. They wanted to lea* it. There was another school that said there must be. What they v interested in was relations with the Americans, and because information came to me via the Americans they also knew that I was a suspect, so there must be exemplary punishment. There were documents that had been circulating in the Berlin station, very sensitive documents, which only a very few people had seen and which reached Moscow. Part of these documents, or some of their contents, had been passed on to the Poles, because it concerned them. When the deputy head of Polish Intelligence defected to the Americans from Berlin, he was able to pass on this information and also give information of Lonsdale [Gordon Lonsdale, former Soviet spy] and Philby. We were not connected, but they followed up the trace and that is how they came to me.' He paused. 'What's the time?' he asked. 'Is it time for us to go to the dacha?'

It was time. I switched off the recording machine. We stood and made our way to the railway station.

*

In the suburban train out of Moscow, we sat opposite each other on the hard wooden seats. Through the window, we viewed the grim industrial landscape. Most countries manage to make a mess of their industrial areas, but the communists seem to have a special talent in this direction. I remember how dismal East Berlin looked compared to the West when I first visited it years ago. Moscow was no exception.

The industrial landscape gradually gave way to open countryside, and as we bumped along I reflected on what my companion had told me. It was an amazing story and I was grateful for the opportunity to talk with him so freely. I hoped we would have a further discussion when we got to the dacha.

After travelling about forty miles or so, the train came to a halt at a small country station.

'We're here,' George said enthusiastically. A tall, handsome young man was waiting for us on the platform and George greeted him warmly. 'This is my son Misha,' he said proudly. We shook hands. Misha spoke perfect English, and we chatted as we walked to a small car. We drove a short distance before leaving the road and entering a thickly wooded area within which were several wooden buildings.

'This,' said George, 'is a dacha. It was not built for people to live in all year round, although there are people who do that. It was built for leasure. I was given this dacha for use only in the summer but then, as like skiing so very much, I was allowed to use it all the year round. In

130

the summer we are mostly here from May until August. Today my wife, one of my sons and my grandson are staying here. I am never here alone.'

'Do you ever spend time alone?' I questioned.

'Yes, in Moscow, and I enjoy that, to tell you the truth. I like classical music and I have good CDs and I like to read very much. In the first years I was offered this dacha, I didn't want it. Then I got married and a child was born, and my wife said that I couldn't refuse, because of my son. The Russians are fresh air fans, you know. Now I like it very much. Previously this dacha would have been occupied by some state official.'

We entered the wooden house. In many respects the building reminded me of the wooden colonial houses built by the settlers across East Africa. In the comfortable living room we were greeted by George's wife Ida, an intelligent and likeable lady who conversed perfectly in English.

She had prepared a meal and we sat at a round table just like any family group enjoying a quiet weekend in the countryside. When we had finished, George and I found a quiet corner to talk.

'Going back now on our previous conversation, are there points you would like to pick up or to expand on further?' I asked.

'Well,' he said, 'we got as far as the Korean War. I spoke about the almost innate anti-Americanism in my make-up.'

'Did you ever voice that to your colleagues in the service?'

'Oh yes, I did. Many shared that view, I think. At that time the CIA was still a fairly new service. There was a certain feeling of superiority in the SIS as being an old and experienced service that had its own ethics. There is one thing in the SIS compared to the CIA and the KGB, and that is the SIS is limited as to the amount of money available, so it has to concentrate its efforts on things it considers really important. It can't afford to cast its net as wide as the CIA and KGB. Of course, they could trade results with the Americans, as they did.'

I wanted George to pick up his narrative once again, so I referred him back to Korea. 'It was in Korea,' I said, 'that you made your first contact and decided to move over to the communist side. Is that correct?'

'Yes, it was exactly fifty years ago,' he answered. 'When we were in Korea and the war broke out we, and the French, had been given instructions to remain in place. But then, because of the American pressure and certain actions of the Soviet representative at the security council a policy was adopted of interfering in the Korean War, which had been planned by the Americans. I spoke to the American G2, who knew well, a very nice man, and a few days before the war broke

131

told me that if there was going to be a war, the line of defence for the Americans was going to be the Japan Sea, between Korea and Japan. They said that the Americans were not going to get involved, and their involvement came as a total surprise. Now, had we known that, we wouldn't have stayed, obviously. But we didn't know. When I got back to England and went to head office and was interviewed by the chief, General Sinclair, he was very nice to me. He said to me, "Oh, what a pity you stayed behind," and I said to him, "But you told me yourself that I should stay!" He then quickly changed the subject.' George laughed at the memory.

After offering his services to the Russians, George was instructed not to do anything, but to wait until he was contacted. This did not take place until he was back in Europe some years later and a meeting was arranged with his Soviet handler in Holland. On this occasion he was routinely followed and almost detected. However, his follower was shaken off and meetings took place thereafter in England, where he began to pass information.

'Was the first information you handed over sensitive?' I asked.

'Yes, it was, very sensitive. My first appointment on returning to England was as deputy head of a new section called Section Y. It was situated in Carlton Gardens opposite the house of the Foreign Secretary. There were a lot of people there of Russian and Polish descent. The job was to process the transcript of tapes that had been obtained from linking up to Soviet military cables. This had started some years earlier and had been so successful that they decided to expand it. At first the information came mainly from Vienna. It was possible, by digging a few tunnels, to get access to these cables. When they began to process the tapes they were so surprised at how much information could be obtained from conversations between military officers talking to one another. But, of course, you had to know Russian extremely well, as they used a lot of slang and there was a great deal of cursing and the like. After the transcribers had obtained the material, it went up higher to British Army officers, who also spoke Russian and who analysed it. Then it was all compiled into a bulletin, which was distributed to the various people who needed to know.'

'So, the Soviet Union would have known from a very early stage that 's was happening?'

'es, that's right.'

d the same with the Berlin tunnel?'

'Yes, I'll tell you about that. On the first or second meeting with my handler in London, I was able to report on the Vienna material and give them a copy of the bulletin. They themselves were astonished at how much could be obtained.' He gave a small chuckle. 'The bulletin was also given to the Americans in the trade-off that I told you about. They were greatly impressed. What happened then was that a treaty was signed and Austria was given its independence. Then, of course, the army withdrew and the listeners withdrew too, so the observation came to an end.

'The man who had organized this was a very good intelligence officer called Peter Lunn. I don't know if you have ever heard of him? His father had the travel agency. Arnold Lunn, I think it was. He was a very nice man, insignificant looking but he spoke very well and was very clever. I think he had something like seven or eight children. He was very respected in the service. When Vienna came to an end, he was appointed to Berlin. Naturally, as the Vienna operation had been so successful, he began to think how he might carry out a similar operation in Berlin. In Berlin the situation was quite different, as the city was divided into sectors and it was much more difficult. He started to study plans of the telephone system and discovered that there were about three points from which one might attack these lines. The point chosen was where three very important Soviet cables ran, but to reach this a tunnel had to be dug for about a hundred and fifty metres, and the tunnel had to be run from the American sector. So the plan couldn't be carried out by the British on their own. They had to bring in the Americans, and not only for that reason. They also could not afford the money needed to carry out an operation of that size. The Americans, having received over a period of time the results of the Vienna operation, were very impressed and agreed to provide the money and some of the technical assistance. They agreed to build some American military installation almost on the border and it would be a cover for the digging of the tunnel.

'It took about a year to plan it all. A mock tunnel was built in England – I think it was somewhere near Salisbury. The soil was very much like the soil in Berlin. In the first meeting, when this whole [?] was discussed, I was there and I could, on a small piece of paper, e[?] where and what was going to be done. Of course, my Soviet [?] number was very impressed and said that he was going t[?] immediately to report it and then we would see what happe[?]

'When he came back he said that they were not going to do anything. They were going to let it happen. They did not tell the KGB people in Berlin. The only man in Berlin who knew was the commander-in-chief of the Soviet forces. And in Moscow there were only a handful of people who knew about this operation. So, they let the tunnel be built and let it run for eleven months.'

'As far as you know, did the Russians transmit false information deliberately to mislead?'

'Transmitting misinformation through the cables is something very, very difficult to do. The telephone lines were connected to real people, officers and so on, and as the operation and counter-operation was so secret, they couldn't warn anybody except to give a general warning, which did not attract any attention. It was more a procedure. It would be very difficult to plant misinformation among that vast amount of genuine information. They allowed this to go on mainly because they were interested in preserving my safety.'

His tone became more serious as he continued his story. 'I must tell you something about the nature of the Cold War,' he said. 'You may already know this. First of all, there was a great deal of military information gathered from the tunnel. But what did the intelligence services on both sides try to find out in the first place? It was this. Both sides suspected the other of wanting to start a war. But each side itself did not intend to do so. The Americans did not intend to attack the Russians, and vice versa. So, what they were looking for was early warning signs of a possible preparation for an atomic war. In this respect the tunnel in East Berlin was very important. It covered the front line of a possible attack, but as the Soviet Union was not planning to attack, it didn't mind so much that it was known it didn't intend to attack.'

Eventually, after eleven months, there was a staged incident when the tunnel was 'discovered' as though by accident and it was opened up by the Russians to be inspected by the press.

'Although,' continued George, 'the Americans played a big part, the equipment and installation was down to the British. The Soviets didn't ᴐention that. They pretended that they believed it was a purely American ·ration. Again, this was to protect myself from discovery.'

ᴐoking back over the years, do you believe that this was the greatest ᴐu communicated?'

was, certainly.'

᠎ others of significance?'

'The others were more accumulative – insight into general methods. How the service worked. What the targets were. They got, over the years, a great deal of information, yes.'

I pressed my question. 'What of significance?'

'There was nothing as significant as the tunnel.'

'And that was only eleven months in running?' I asked.

'Yes, eleven months. Both sides considered it to be a triumph. The British did get very considerable information and the Russians had the last word, as it were. This was the only giant CIA–SIS operation in which I was directly involved.'

'Was this why you were given such a long sentence?'

'Yes, I believe it was. The main purpose was to show the Americans that the British were not going to tolerate that kind of activity. Philby was warned not to come back to the UK when he was in Beirut. Blunt was interrogated and then let off and allowed to keep his position as Keeper of the Queen's Pictures in order to avoid a scandal. Only later was this discovered by the press and then the authorities had to admit it.

'I didn't know about Blunt, nor about Maclean and Burgess, although I knew about them when I came back from Korea. They were all over the place. They had just escaped. Philby also I never met until years later in Russia.'

'Looking back on all of these different experiences, how do you evaluate your life?'

'That's a very difficult question. I have to think about it.'

We sat in silence for a while before he continued.

'How do I evaluate my life from my own point of view?'

'Yes.'

'I think it was not a wasted life. I think it was a very interesting life which gave me experiences for which I am very grateful. I was put in a very unusual position and, in that respect, I have no regrets. I have, of course, caused harm to many people.'

'Who specifically?'

'Well, in the first place my family, though they have come out of it well. Also, you touched on it previously, the matter of deceiving people. That' not something of which one can be very proud. That's on a purely pers level. I didn't like to deceive. It wasn't something I got pleasure o have never felt any great indignation at my sentence or my pun I don't know what I would have felt if I had spent over twe prison and then come out. As it worked out I don't feel any

'Do you think your activities contributed in any way to peace?'

'Well, for a certain period, as anything in intelligence is only for a limited period, I think it helped both sides to become convinced that the other was not going to attack, and that was very important. I don't place myself in the very high category of the atomic spies. I think they helped towards avoiding the unleashing of atomic war. I think we owe them gratitude in that respect. I know there are many people who would disagree with that, but that is my own opinion. Of course, I knew these people, at least some of them. Donald Maclean was involved in atomic spying – and the Krogers. They were people of exceptionally high moral standards. I know that most people in England who heard me say this would be very much surprised. But it is a fact.'

Again, he fell silent for a moment.

'Would you recommend taking up a career in intelligence to any of your own children?' I asked.

He answered immediately. 'No, I wouldn't. First of all, I don't think any of them would have the disposition for the work, and my son Misha, who loves me and respects me – I don't think he would like to imitate me.'

I then asked him a question about solitude, from which none of us can escape: 'We are both in the last quarter of life, one might say. How do you view the supreme point of solitude, death?'

'Well, I am not afraid of death. I hope that I shall be able to pass on peacefully.'

'Do you believe in an afterlife?'

'In that respect I am open. I don't want to say there is no afterlife. Also, I don't want to say there is. I don't know. If I were to die tonight I would feel that I have had a very worthwhile life.'

'Let me put to you this question. If tonight the gate to your dacha were suddenly to open and through it came many of your former colleagues from SIS, is there anything you would want to say to them?'

'Well, I suppose I would say the sort of thing I have been saying to you. I think I would be able to talk to them and establish a good relationship with them. My last talks with my former SIS colleagues were, in ⌐t, on a very understanding basis. There is one thing about the secret ⸱ces, of course – they deal in treason. That is their business and they ⸱xist otherwise. On the other hand, they fear treason more than ⸱ else. That inner contradiction never resolves itself. The discus- ⸱ having is largely academic now, but there may well be a time ⸱ of the world when something similar will happen again.'

It was at this point that our recorded discussion ended. Later, Misha, accompanied by his father, drove us back to Moscow, where I returned to my hotel.

Of all the major defectors of that time – Blake, Burgess, Maclean and Philby – George Blake appears to be the one who was able to accommodate himself to life in the Soviet Union without too much difficulty. That is what he implied to me and I have little doubt that it is true. The meeting with George Blake gave me a fascinating insight into the mind of a complex individual. I don't believe for one moment that he told me the whole story concerning his escape. He may not even know it himself. However, I don't believe that he was at any point lying to me.

It was after writing the account of our conversation in Moscow that I recalled a further story he told me when we were not being recorded.

When he was in the Scrubs, he had smuggled into his cell a small two-way radio that enabled him to communicate with those people planning his escape on the outside. Each night he would have a brief conversation with his helpers over the wall. One morning, a fellow prisoner came into his cell and pushed the door to.

'George,' he said, excitedly. 'What the hell are you doing?'

George looked blank and asked what he meant.

'Last night,' continued the prisoner, 'I was listening to my radio when I heard a voice cutting across the programme. At first I thought it was a play or documentary on another channel, but as I listened I realized it was your voice! Your signal is being picked up on an ordinary radio.'

'Do you know,' Blake told me, 'that man never gave me away. No one ever found out about the radio.'

One characteristic that struck me following my conversation with George Blake was that deception seemed to be almost built into his genetic background. His father concealed his Jewishness, and the young George kept in the shadows when, as a very young man, he was working as a runner in the resistance movement.

On one occasion I asked him how he felt about being called a traitor to his country, the UK. He replied, 'To be a traitor you have to belong never belonged.'

From the solitude that is part and parcel of each and eve of us, he built a web of deception, reinforced by his religio which emphasized equality and fair sharing. I suspect, and suspicion, that his more hardline Calvinistic beliefs only later life, when they could be used to provide justification for his life and actions.

*

A couple of years after my meeting with Blake, I returned to Moscow to attend a conference. Before I left London, I was in touch with him again and arranged to see him once more, as there were a number of follow-up questions I wanted to ask him. It was arranged that, on my arrival in the city, I would telephone him and he would then suggest a location for us to meet.

One morning I telephoned him from my hotel.

'I'm sorry,' he said, 'I have a dental appointment, so I can't meet today.'

'I'll phone you tomorrow,' I replied.

The next morning we spoke again and he told me he was far from well and would not be able to meet. As I was due to leave Russia the following day there was no chance of meeting him. Russia was now under the control of Vladimir Putin and I suspect, although I have no proof, that Blake had been warned off. That was the last contact I had with him.

Part 3

INESCAPABLE SOLITUDE

'Lana Peters will be coming to dinner next week. Would you like to meet her?'

The name meant nothing to me, so I asked who she might be.

'You probably know her best as Svetlana Alliluyeva,' was the reply and, of course, I recognized the name immediately. I had read one of her books, *Twenty Letters to a Friend*, and through this knew something of her ambivalent relationship with her late father, Joseph Stalin. Alas, I was returning from my brief stay in New York to London the following day so, to my regret, could not accept. As it happened, that was not to be the end of the matter.

Several weeks after returning to London, my friend in the USA contacted me again regarding Svetlana, or Lana as she preferred to be called.

'She will be coming to the United Kingdom soon, where she hopes to settle. Do you think you might be able to help her find accommodation?'

To cut a long story short, one morning a middle-aged lady carrying a small suitcase arrived at our south London home, where we had prepared a room for her to use until she was able to get some longer-term accommodation. She had separated from her American lawyer husband, William Peters, and was caring for her teenage daughter, Olga.

Lana's two years spent in the UK are barely documented. Following her death, a review of her life published in *Time* magazine does not mention it at all. In an interview that she gave in 1983, she is quoted as saying: 'Over me my father's shadow hovers, no matter what I do or say.'

That unique and indeed terrible inheritance produced in her an understandable inner loneliness and an uncomfortable solitude.

One January, at Orthodox Christmas, she said that she would like to go to the Russian church in London that I attended from time to time. I said that I would be more than happy to go along with her, and at first she agreed. Then she changed her mind.

12 Svetlana, daughter of Stalin

'I can't bring myself to go,' she said sadly. 'Many of those people have been exiled by my father and they would know me. I can't face them.'

Not surprisingly, Lana had difficulty in maintaining long-term relationships and trusting people. In an interview she once said, 'I don't trust anyone or anything. If he [Stalin] could kill so many people, including my uncles and aunties, I will never forgive him. Never.'

I was warned. 'Be careful,' more than one person said to me. 'She has a habit of eventually turning against those who attempt to help her.' There were many people in the UK who gave her valuable assistance in finding accommodation and getting settled. The late Malcolm Muggeridge was one and, true to form, Lana fell out with him, and others.

It was not too long before I came into the firing line. She wanted Olga, her daughter by Peters, to come over to the UK and be educated here. I made several enquiries on her behalf, and one Easter Sunday morning the three of us set off to see the headmaster of the Quaker school in Saffron Waldron. He had kindly made time available, even though it was a holiday. The interviews took place and Olga went to the school as a boarder.

Later, Lana criticized me for recommending a school that had 'corrupted' her daughter! I don't mean in any way to be patronizing, but I would genuinely say, 'Poor Olga.' She too had to live with the legacy left to the world by her grandfather, and was also a prisoner of his name and inheritance. Today she lives in the USA and has changed her name.

Her mother had a nomadic spirit, and although she was eventually found a good house in Cambridge, where she was surrounded by discreet and good friends, she could not settle. She would frequently say to me that she had a strong desire to return to Georgia in the Soviet Union. I did not try to stop her in any way, but I warned her that I doubted she would find the happiness she was seeking there. However, she was determined.

One day I called to see her in Cambridge and found the house firmly secured and empty. She had gone. Soon I learned that she had returned to her home and, as I expected, it was not long before she was on the move once more. I never saw her again.

I am including this very brief snapshot to illustrate one point about ⸱de. An individual can find themselves trapped and isolated through ⸱ely no fault of their own, but because of their inheritance. That ⸱an, and does, pass down the generations and it deeply influ-
's life, as it also affected Olga's.

Some years ago a judge who was certified to try sex cases came to see me. He had been a friend for many years. During the course of our conversation he mentioned that he was becoming increasingly depressed.

'I am so overburdened with unpleasant sex cases involving children,' he said, 'that I am in danger of developing a warped impression of all human beings.'

Being a mature and sensible individual, he coped with the problem, but I could well understand his difficulty. I myself find it virtually impossible to read details of certain cases that involve abuse of children. Although I have been told about the terrible torture inflicted on young children by Ian Brady and Myra Hindley, I have not read the details, nor have I any intention of doing so. The Moors Murders, as they were called in the 1960s when Brady and Hindley collaborated in the torture and murder of five young people, will go down as one of the most horrific crimes in British history.

I first met Myra Hindley in Durham, where she was serving a life sentence. (This prison is now closed.) When I visited, the prison housed both men and women, but because of severe overcrowding and several suicides, it became a men-only establishment in 2005.

Myra Hindley was living in the women's wing in H block, alongside Rosemary West and others. West was convicted, with her husband, of committing a number of dreadful murders at their home in Gloucestershire and received several whole life sentences. Later I visited Myra Hindley in the segregation wing at Highpoint Prison in Suffolk.

In British prisons, segregation does not mean that a prisoner is kept in total isolation. They can converse with prison officers and normally have access to television, radio, books and magazines.

Myra Hindley was seen by many to be an icon of evil. This perception was not improved by the fact that when her name appeared in the press it was frequently accompanied by a photograph that portrayed her as a fairly young woman, and was not the most flattering of pictures.

I met her many years after the photograph was taken. She had the sallow complexion that is so common with prisoners, was somewhat overweight and was suffering from high blood pressure and osteoporosis. She smoked heavily, which did not in any way help with her health problems.

I visited her many times across the years and, without in any way minimizing her crimes, I am fairly confident that the remorse she expressed to me on more than one occasion was genuine. She had become a convert to Roman Catholicism in her youth and it was clear that she had received considerable help from the RC prison chaplains, of whom she spoke most highly.

The murders she committed with Ian Brady took place when she was barely out of her teens. It is my belief that, as a young woman, she fell under the spell cast by Ian Brady and would do virtually anything he asked of her. It is certainly not uncommon for a young woman to become totally infatuated with a man and lose all reason. Brady was declared to be mentally ill many years after his conviction and was then committed to a secure hospital.

I had a number of conversations with her, when she expressed her remorse and desire to be released on parole. I felt that release was most unlikely for several reasons. First, as I said earlier, the media had made her into an icon of evil, and although there were regrettably many others who had committed equally horrific crimes, no politician was going to risk votes by authorizing her release. Second, had she been released she would have been in real danger of losing her life. 'I would be willing to take that risk,' she said to me more than once.

Myra Hindley, like Lana Peters, experienced a particular form of solitude. The fact that she had participated in such dreadful crimes in the past isolated her from other prisoners and put her into a terrible form of isolation and solitude. In Lana's case her father's crimes, not her own, followed her to the grave and she could never free herself or be freed from the past. Myra Hindley was also trapped, but by her own actions, and they imprisoned her for life. Had she been released from prison they would still have followed her and she would have remained trapped. Her actions, along with those of Brady, had also trapped the relatives of her unfortunate victims. For the remainder of their lives they would experience a deep, inner, solitary agony. Solitude of this kind is the solitude of alienation. It leads to death and despair unless it is redeemed.

As I was writing this book, an old friend of mine died. He represented the last of a generation who had personal experience of the horrors of the Japanese prisoner-of-war camps.

At the outbreak of the Second World War, Harold Lock was a young teenager. He was not exactly truthful about his age, and when he was fifteen he volunteered for the Royal Navy. He was accepted and, after a brief spell of training, found himself serving on board HMS *Jupiter*, a destroyer sailing off the coast of Indonesia. In January 1942, during what became known as the Battle of the Java Sea, *Jupiter* sank a Japanese submarine, but ironically, the following month, on 27 February, she struck a mine that had recently been laid by the Dutch minelayer *Gouden Leeuw*. *Jupiter* sank off the north Java coast in the Java Sea and it was thought at the time that the explosion brought about by the mine was caused by a Japanese torpedo. *Jupiter* went down, with the loss of many lives.

Harold, being young and fit, was able to swim the twelve or so miles to land, where he was immediately captured by the invading Japanese. He was handed a spade and told to begin digging his grave. While he was digging, fully believing that his life was about to end, he heard a voice behind him say, in perfect English, 'You're in a fine mess, aren't you?'

He turned around to see that the voice belonged to a Japanese officer. He learned later that this man had lived in the USA for many years, had returned to Japan and been conscripted into the army.

'I can't get you out of this completely,' continued the officer, 'as you will have to go to a camp, but at least your life will be spared.'

It has been recorded that out of a total crew of one hundred and ninety-two officers and men, ninety-five died during the sinking, ninety-seven men survived and twenty-seven of these died during their captivity.

The next three years, from 1942 to 1945, were spent in Japanese prisoner-of-war camps centred around what is now Jakarta. All in all he spent time in four camps, the most severe of which was Huruku, where he stayed until the end of the war.

I first met Harold many years ago when I became a patron of my local branch of the Far Eastern Prisoners of War Association (FEPOW). There was a flourishing branch in Suffolk and I joined them on many an occasion, sadly watching as each year their number diminished. They were without doubt a wonderful group of men and I have very many good memories of being with them and their families for the social occasions and commemorative events in which they participated.

At the end of hostilities, and after a short period of recuperation in Australia, Harold was brought home on a troop carrier. On docking, he received a small sum of money, some civilian clothing and was told not to talk about his experience but to get on with his life. This instruction was given to most, if not all, returning prisoners at that time. They received what medical help they needed, but any form of counselling assistance was not considered at all necessary. It has been said, by some uninformed critics of post-traumatic stress counselling, that the returning prisoners from the Second World War managed perfectly well, so why should later generations need this form of help? The fact is that some of those returning did manage well, but there were substantial numbers who did not.

After becoming associated with FEPOW, I was invited to become a patron of COFEPOW. This is an organization for the Children & Families of the Far Eastern Prisoners of War. I heard from many of them how, following the return of their father from the camps, often things were not easy at home. The vast majority of former captives obeyed, to the letter, the injunction not to speak about their experiences, and simply buried these dreadful memories deep down in their subconscious. This was also partly due to a 'stiff upper lip' mentality, as many of the returnees would not have wished to unduly upset their wives and children with stories of their captivity. It is often the case that when a traumatic experience is not dealt with as soon as possible following the event, then it makes its appearance in middle life through flashbacks, dreams and nightmares. Many family members told me of the difficulties their fathers experienced and the strain put upon them as time went ·y. Today, combat stress, and the like, is recognized and in many cases ·quate therapeutic treatment is given when required.

·any of the former captives found themselves locked into an unusual f solitude. They obeyed orders and buried their experience, with ·lt that severe communication problems developed in many families. Both FEPOW and COFEPOW have played a highly significant role in aiding former captives and their families to cope with these issues.

*

One day, when Harold had just turned eighty, he came to see me.

'I've been thinking,' he said. 'I'm getting on, and before I die I would like to return to the place where our ship went down all those years ago.'

I listened to him carefully.

'I don't think there is much of a chance. My wife won't fly and it would be a very expensive journey.'

'Well, Harold,' I replied, 'let's see what can be done.'

When he had gone, I asked Sarah, my secretary, to contact the Admiralty in London and find the exact coordinates for where Harold's ship was sunk. I then set about looking into airfares so that both he and I could make the journey together. Meanwhile Sarah made some bookings for accommodation and in no time at all Harold and I were at Heathrow airport in London preparing to board a flight for the first leg of our journey to Singapore.

'I've never flown before,' Harold confessed, 'so I asked my doctor to give me something for the flight.'

'Forget the pills, Harold,' I said, somewhat recklessly. 'We are travelling Business Class, so try the champagne instead!'

I had arranged for us to spend a couple of days in Singapore so that we could visit the prisoner-of-war museum near to Changi airport, which of course was the site of that notorious prison camp of the Second World War. We walked around the exhibition in silence, gazing at the pictures of those poor souls who had suffered so dreadfully. Harold began to recount some of the stories from his past. How an Australian doctor, himself a captive, had operated and performed amputations without the aid of anaesthetic. How the prisoners had been able to construct a small chapel in which the padre (another captive, of course) took simple services. He also told me about the lesser known side of camp life, when prisoners who had collaborated with the Japanese were 'dealt with'. He left it at that.

We arrived in Indonesia and checked into the simple hotel on the same island where Harold had first been incarcerated over sixty years earlier. We made some inquiries and, as luck would have it, discovere a local man who, when we showed him the map, knew exactly wh Harold's ship had gone down.

'It sank in shallow water,' he said, 'and we can see the mast at low tide. It's still there.'

He agreed to take us the next day, so we went back into the small town and had a simple wreath made.

Next morning there was a slight wind, and the sea was quite choppy, but we made our way down to the beach and boarded the small vessel by first of all wading through the water and then clambering over the side. Harold sat silently clutching the floral tribute that we had had made. No doubt a thousand memories were flooding through his mind as we made our pilgrimage to the watery grave of his former shipmates.

Then we were there. As I stood by his side, Harold took hold of the wreath and, following a few moments of silence, threw it into the waters. We watched as it gently bobbed up and down in the ocean.

We continued to be alone with our thoughts as we returned to the shore to make the long journey home.

*

It will only be a very short time before the last of the survivors of the camps will have died. For several years they shared a common life together, and on their return home that experience was buried on the instructions of their superiors. They experienced an unusual form of solitude. Once they returned to civilian life, this communal life became a solitary experience that they were unable to share with those who were closest to them. Eventually many were able to come to terms with this. Some were not.

When I visited Ted, the former SIS operative and later accomplished author, I knew something of his background and the unusual form of solitude he had experienced in his work. As we spoke, I discovered that he was experiencing a new form of solitude: that of a carer; one who, day after day, cares for a relative or a friend and in some measure experiences the strain of that commitment.

His experience was of particular interest to me as for several years my sister had been caring for our elderly mother, whom we had seen gradually slip into the solitude of senility. During the same week that I met Ted in Kent, I travelled to the north of England, to the village where I was born. My purpose was to talk to Margaret, the former matron of a hospice, who had recently retired and was adjusting to a new form of life. I wanted to talk with her about death, and the particular solitude of that experience.

It had been over forty years since I had visited this small Cheshire village to which my parents had moved just before I was born. There, on the hill, stood my parents' first home. My father had been dead for many years and my mother was now at a stage where she barely recognized any of her three children. Now, I stood on the very spot where they started life together full of hope for the future. My mind returned to my childhood, as it frequently had when I was incarcerated. I can never return to my roots without feeling powerful emotions.

I returned to the car and drove to the outskirts of the village to meet my next interviewee. It was a lovely sunny day and Margaret was waiting for me in her garden. She was now into her second week of retirement and still coming to terms with the experience.

'It's not unlike a bereavement,' she said, as she arranged a couple of chairs around a small table. 'You feel the loss and, for the past couple of weeks, I have been quite lethargic.'

Earlier in the year I had attended her retirement dinner, where many tributes were paid to her for her years of selfless dedication. Then I had asked her if she knew how many patients had passed through the hospice during her time as matron. She couldn't be exact, but she thought it was about seventeen hundred.

We sat down and she continued. 'I left the hospice on the Friday. It was all very emotional. On the Saturday I went to my god-daughter's wedding in Coventry Cathedral and afterwards we went for a reception at Burnt Norton, which is now a derelict house. We had some poetry readings and walked around the garden. It was unusual but very nice.'

The place, Burnt Norton, reminded me of T. S. Eliot and some words from his poem of the same name. In this well-known poem he speaks of the complexity of time. How the end and the beginning are always present and yet everything is constantly changing. It was strangely appropriate to recall this in a week of different journeys.

'On the Sunday morning I felt very sad and emotional,' she continued, 'and a friend rang me up. She had a minor medical problem and she asked me if I would mind holding her baby at a christening. That was wonderful and I felt so much better afterwards.

'The hospice philosophy is to allow people to die with dignity. If possible to be at peace with their God and with man. The measure by which we achieve that depends to a certain extent on the time we have. I've always wanted to have someone be with the patient while they are dying, but I'm afraid that is being eroded today because of the workload. You can't always do that these days.'

During her nursing career, both with the hospice movement and elsewhere, Margaret had been with hundreds of people who were at the point of death. She spoke about this.

'I've had various experiences across my nursing career which have enlightened me about the way people approach death. It's a journey they have to make alone, but only beyond the point of being in physical touch with the world. That's very difficult to define. How do we know? We don't. I remember one deeply devout lady. She had planned everything for the family, even her husband's remarriage. When it came to her last moments, her husband came to see me and said, "She's ready to go, but won't come for her." I was a young ward sister at the time and I went ‎ her, although I really didn't know what to do. I said, "Just lean back ‎ the pillow and close your eyes, and he will come." She did so and ‎in minutes. I think that many individuals need permission to ‎e. They leave behind their partners of many years, or perhaps ‎ly. Strangely, in many cases it doesn't seem to grieve those who leave a young family so much. They are able to see a purpose and a future for them. A partner left behind is often desolate, and frequently sees no reason for continuing life.'

She paused and remained silent for a moment. 'It's the young who particularly need permission to die. They fight. They will try every avenue of alternative medicine and will be angry that the treatment hasn't worked and the disease is overcoming them. On the other hand, it's so very sad when you meet people who believe there is nothing worth staying on this earth for. I remember a widow in her forties who shot herself with a sawn-off shotgun. When she awoke after five hours of surgery she was very angry, and naturally I was more than anxious for her during the recovery period. Twenty-five years later she came into the hospice dying of cancer. After a week I told her that I had nursed her all those years ago. We were able to talk about it together with her family. She had eventually found some meaning in life by supporting her daughters through their marital problems. Was she afraid of being alone or was it the purposelessness of it all that she experienced?'

Once again she lapsed into silence. 'It is very difficult to be with some-one who is dying and to try and accompany them as far as you can. There is a feeling of ineptitude. I'm not talking professionally. I'm talking about the families, the carers. They feel so helpless, and for many, just to sit holding a hand is not enough. I realized this in particular when my own mother died here in this house. She needed to get her breath and I had to sit behind her to support her in an upright position. I couldn't hold her hand, nor could I move to go and get help. It was all over in a few minutes and then there is that feeling of helplessness that you can't go with them or help them any further. They have to face it alone, and you can't go that far, even with your own family.

'I think it's important for the carer to have someone else around as well. I remember a friend of mine saying she was alone in a private room with her father who was choking to death. He was dying and she felt totally bereft. She felt that the world had forgotten her and that she was totally helpless. No one was coming to help *her*, to support *her*. Solitude is in the actual journey, because only those who are dying know what they are feeling. They are on that journey, not you, not anybody who is listening to them. They are on that journey. You can accompany them so far, but no further. Whether their journey is one of calm and peace depends to a large extent on their beliefs. Belief does a difference to the way people approach death and how they die.'

151

As Margaret was speaking, I couldn't get out of my mind the fact that she had been with so many people as they embarked on their last solitary journey. I wondered about the effect on her of living constantly with death.

'It's the concentration really. When you're in the more active kind of nursing, there are so many other priorities to see to and it's very seldom that you have the privilege of sharing in someone's death. When I went to the hospice, one of the first things I instituted was commendation prayers. When I was with somebody who had just died I wanted to send them on their way with a blessing, and I felt that it was important that the nurses had a tool to help them with the family bereavement. There were some families, of course, who didn't want prayers said at all, and we always respected their wishes, but the prayers were also for our support. To meet our need as carers. Grieving is synonymous with caring. Caring is synonymous with love. If you are going to care, then you are going to grieve. You must do so. I learned that lesson very early, with a young man of twenty-nine who died. I had left instructions after my shift that if the staff wanted me, I would come back. When I was called back, the staff were in some disarray. They were very tearful. They could deal with the death of the young man, but not with the family. So I did that. Later in the day one of the domestic staff came to me and asked if I realized how very upset they had been in the kitchen. I hadn't realized. I had forgotten that group of people who, in a hospice environment, cared and because they cared they were grieving.

'There was a time when we used to attend every funeral, but that didn't last for long. We couldn't cope with it. I had to explain to the staff that we all had to work within the limits of our emotional resources. I remember once when one of the night staff had a death on each of her three nights of duty and I felt that was a little disproportionate compared to what the others had experienced. When I spoke with her she hesitated for a moment and then said, "Yes, it was hard, but each death was beautiful." So, from that point of view, dealing with the actual death is the culmination of years of experience and the staff are able to put their experience into practice and help the patient achieve a good death.'

We continued to speak about the effect of the death of a patient on the ⸱ilies, and on others in the ward. Margaret admitted that it was increas- difficult to give sufficient time to the families, who do require a lot and understanding both before and after the death. She said that hospitals, at the time of death curtains were drawn around the bedside. There were times in the hospice when the patient died in full view of others in the ward. Rather than shock and disturb the other patients, it brought them some consolation to see that death could be peaceful.

I asked Margaret about her own approach to solitude and how she coped with the solitude of responsibility.

'I am, at heart, a solitary person. I enjoy my own company, so long as I can get out and meet with other people from time to time. But now that I have retired, I shall miss the patients. I believe that love does change everything. There is a saying, "The way you live, the way you die." I believe that. As for the responsibilities of the job, well, I did resort to seeing a counsellor at one stage. It was at a time of management difficulties and I felt that I was not equipped to make all the management decisions that I was being asked to make. The counsellor was good. Before, I'd always been wary of that sort of thing, but she allowed me to put things into perspective and work out my priorities.

'In employing nurses, I always thought that it was important they should have faced the question of their own death. I also wanted those who had life experience, as well as professional experience. I wanted to know about their religion. If they were religious or not was not material, but I needed to sort out the fanatics. Many years ago I had a big row with someone who was delivering leaflets to my patients and reducing them to tears. That was not acceptable in the hospice. I couldn't have that; it wasn't right.

'I am happy on my own, although I realize that living alone can make you very selfish. Solitude is different from loneliness. Solitude that is self-centred cannot be satisfying. I think that the lonely have to care about other people and not just about themselves. If they develop an outside interest of some kind they can perhaps ease their own loneliness. I don't think you deliberately choose loneliness. You can choose solitude.'

With my sister and Ted still very much in mind, I returned to the subject of the sick and the dying.

Margaret said, 'People who live close to death for a long period of time don't necessarily lose their fear of it. Carers can get a false sense of security when things go on for so long, and when eventually death comes, it can be a great shock. As for those who are ill and still retain their mental faculties, short-term targets can be important. I remembe all sorts of examples. The young man who wanted to go abroad to m his mother before he died; the lady whose daughter was expecting a and she hung on and on until the baby was born. We all shared joy when she was with us for the baptism in the hospice chapel.

died a few days later. If there is a target people want to achieve, they often seem to be able to delay death by an act of will.'

It was approaching lunchtime and we went indoors. For the next hour or so we relaxed, after the intensity of the morning. Margaret spoke about the future of the hospice movement and its provision of places of comfort, hope *and* joy for those who are embarking on their final solitary journey. She remarked that so many people when they first go to a hospice are surprised to find that they are places of laughter and happiness. She was concerned for the future.

'I always believed,' she said, 'that British nurses were the best trained in the world, and they continue to be very good. But I fear our standards have been lowered in recent years. As for hospice work, it might be absorbed into palliative care and become much more generalized. Then it would lose its specialty and perhaps its charitable status. I hope we don't lose the unique contribution we can, and do, make to our patients.'

Who but the most callous would not agree with that? A hospice is unique in so many ways, not least because the patients, family, friends and staff can, and do, face the truth of death, and in so doing find the truth to be wholesome and healing. What is more, they have the opportunity to face and live the truth together with compassion. The reality of solitude faced at the point of death is the reality that is with us throughout the whole of life. Others can be with us intimately, but there is always some deep, solitary point within us. In life we may deny it, but death, the ultimate reality, has no space for denial.

I said goodbye to Margaret, climbed into the car and drove slowly through the lanes of my childhood. Any patients who died in the hospice that night would have the opportunity to die peacefully and truthfully.

When I returned home I looked at Shakespeare, for as usual he had a wise word to offer:

> Of all the wonders that I have heard,
> It seems to me most strange that men should fear;
> Seeing death, a necessary end,
> Will come when it will come.
>
> (*Julius Caesar*, Act 2 Scene 2)

We arrived at Yaroslavsky railway station soon after 11 p.m. It was Orthodox New Year and that evening we had been to a performance of *The Nutcracker* at the Bolshoi Theatre in Moscow. This was the final performance before the theatre was to be closed for extensive repairs and it was packed out for what was a glittering performance. As soon as the ballet was over we quickly hailed a cab and made directly for the railway terminal, from which our train departed shortly before midnight. Earlier in the day we had descended on a Moscow supermarket and filled two very large wicker hampers with provisions for the journey, having been told that the dining car on the Trans-Siberian Railway was to be avoided at all costs! We were a party of eight and had booked four adjacent double compartments on the ordinary service train bound for Beijing.

A porter collected our luggage, together with the hampers, from the left luggage kiosk, loaded them on to a trolley and set off at a brisk pace to find our reserved seats. It was starting to snow and we were more than happy when, having been greeted by the two attendants for our carriage, we stepped into the warm interior that was to be our home for the next seven days. Before we had even seen our compartment we slipped them both a few dollars, as they would be in charge of our welfare for the next week, and we wanted to start off on the right foot!

At one end of the carriage was a large samovar, which supplied constant hot water for the whole journey. At the other end the toilets were situated. They were primitive, to say the least, but they had to suffice. The compartment allocated to us was certainly adequate, and each night the attendant would come and make up two beds and return them to comfortable seats the following morning. So, once settled, we were in a warm and secure place to observe a landscape that is inseparably linked with the hardships of solitude: Siberia.

One of the most descriptive books I have read about tracking through Siberia is by the Pole Slavomir

Rawicz. At the outbreak of the Second World War he was sentenced by the Russians to twenty-five years' forced labour in a Siberian prison camp. In his book *The Long Walk*, he claims to have escaped. There is some doubt as to the authenticity of this claim, but his description of the terrain and the hardship endured, when being forcibly herded across it by the Russian Army, are real enough and literally utterly chilling.

It was in the mid-eighteenth century that the Russian government first sent criminals and political opponents to Eastern Siberia. It could take anything up to three years to travel to their destination and many died en route, which may well have been the hope of the government. A part of the railway on which I was travelling had been constructed by prisoners who worked in the most appalling conditions. Later on, people were exiled to this remote region in an attempt to populate it and work in the mines and forests.

I won't attempt to give a blow-by-blow description of our journey. Suffice to say that when we woke on the first morning we were well away from civilization and already beginning to plunge deep into the heart of this remote territory. We could see for miles across vast snowy wastes and then, suddenly as if from nowhere, we spotted a lone figure plodding a solitary way through the drifts. Slowly the plains gave way to mountainous regions and then came Lake Baikal, frozen solid and reputed to be the deepest lake in the world.

Here I was reminded of the French adventurer Sylvain Tesson, who left his home in Paris and stayed alone for six months in a cabin by the lake. He was some six days' walk away from the nearest village and at least a day from his nearest neighbour. He made an interesting observation in a newspaper article:

> People who live in cabins can quickly fall into a state of depression, of cabin fever . . . Nobody will say anything to you. So it's important to organise your time with activity, like the monks did; or Robinson Crusoe, who dressed for dinner every night though he was shipwrecked and alone. The way to stay smart is to behave when you are alone as you would surrounded by people in the city.

The need to organize one's time, which he recognized, was exactly what I discovered during my years of enforced solitude. In the first week of my captivity I had my own clothes and at night I would remove my trousers and place them under my mattress on the floor in order to keep them as neatly pressed as I could. My captors thought I was totally mad, but that was my equivalent of dressing for dinner.

His comments about elemental forces also fascinated me:

> When the ice broke on 22 May, it happened suddenly: there was a storm and the ice shattered. I have never seen such power. It was like the elements were making war. In the West we talk about the beginning of spring, of entering spring. In Siberia there was no entering, no transition; it was rapid. In ten minutes winter was defeated.

To live with the solitude of such places one has to be able to enter into a relationship with the forces of nature. It is in such places that one realizes, and learns to respect, the power and the beauty of the world. As I have said earlier in this book, many people today have lost contact with nature and appear to be at war with it. We cover the earth with concrete and alienate ourselves from the elemental forces that have the power to create or destroy.

As we crossed Siberia, I reflected on other solitary regions of the world I had visited. The Sahara Desert – climatically exactly opposite to this territory, but with a beauty all of its own. The Amazon jungle – vast, remote and in some respects quite frightening. The Antarctic – strangely silent until the wind stirs before mustering with devastating force.

The solitude of the earth relates to the solitude within. The remote regions of this world have a harmony of their own. We need to be able to relate to that solitude. A part of the secret of inner harmony is to face solitude squarely and enter into the harmony that is a part of the music of creation.

In the Prelude to this book, I mentioned the classic work on solitude by Anthony Storr, entitled *Solitude*. In a chapter in that book, when the author discusses enforced solitude, he examines brainwashing and the techniques deployed to extract information.

In my conversations with George Blake in Moscow, I asked him if he was subject to such techniques and he strongly denied that he was. He did say, however, that it was during the time of his captivity in North Korea that he made his decision to offer his services to the Russians. He seemed to be reluctant to speak in detail about the time he spent in captivity and thus there is still a small element of doubt in my mind as to how he was treated. It is virtually certain that Blake, as a young man, was greatly influenced by his cousin in Egypt and that his sympathies for the communist cause had been developing over the years. Korea may well have given him the final push.

Storr refers to an experiment when volunteers were confined to a darkened, soundproofed room and required to lie still for most of the time. As this was an experiment, volunteers were, of course, allowed to terminate the process at any time.

In the main, those who undertook the experiment suffered from reduced intellectual performance, especially if they were required to engage in creative activity. Their ability to concentrate suffered and in some cases they were plagued by constant obsessional thoughts over which they had little or no control. A number of volunteers surrendered almost completely to daydreaming.

One of the most interesting results of these experiments was that some volunteers became eight times more susceptible to propaganda compared to subjects tested under normal conditions. Hallucination and panic attacks, along with irrational fears, were observed, and one volunteer demanded early release as his mind became full of unpleasant childhood memories that drove him to distraction.

I have seen this experience repeated many times in civilian prisons in the UK. One particular instance comes to mind of a young woman I met in a British jail. Her arms were deeply scarred as a result of multiple attempts at self-harm. She was kept alone in a cell for long periods, during which time she relived, in her mind, childhood experiences when she was constantly abused. The pain she inflicted on herself by cutting her arms was her way of blotting out such memories from her consciousness.

As for my own experience of solitary confinement, when I was totally alone for month after month, I remember being plagued by unpleasant and disturbing memories from my past. At times they almost drove me to distraction and it took a considerable act of will to try and find some inner balance. I had to learn to discipline my imagination, and this I did, in part, by writing in my head. This was the only means open to me, as I was without pencil and paper throughout captivity. I also had to recognize that, in company with all human beings, I was a complex mixture of 'Light and Dark', and I needed to be realistic about my nature and not be over-depressed when the dark side loomed. I thought that the brief account of the few weeks I spent in South Africa worth recording here as, although mercifully I was not overcome by depression, I was totally unable to engage in any creative writing. This illustrates that solitude is by no means an open door to creativity or to peace. It can be very hard work. I have the deepest sympathy for those who suffer from depression. It is an awful condition.

The late Arthur Koestler wrote a collection of essays entitled *Kaleidoscope*, and in the final chapter of his book, Storr mentions the dialogue recorded between Koestler and Anthony Grey. Grey was imprisoned in China, where he experienced solitary confinement, and Koestler was in solitary imprisonment in Spain.

Although I have read many of Koestler's writings, I never met him, but I did meet Grey. I rather regret now that we were unable to have a significant discussion about his solitary experience, but at the time of our meeting he appeared to be obsessed with his investigations into UFOs and I was not particularly interested in that subject. Koestler remarked in his book that there was a danger of reducing the experience of solitary confinement by 'talking it away'. One tended, he said, to become either maudlin or too intellectualized. Both Grey and Koestler said that they were grateful not to have had to share a cell with others. Grey remarked, 'I felt I had only myself to deal with. I felt that I could deal with myself but I couldn't necessarily control someone else.' Koestler responded by saying that oneself is already a handful, implying that that was quite enough for him to deal with. Both felt that their experience deepened their sympathy and understanding of other human beings.

Their experience links with my own. I only shared a cell with others for the last few weeks of captivity and, for a whole variety of reasons, found that a strain. Having spent years totally alone, it was not easy to resume interpersonal communications, especially when we were all under considerable stress. On the other hand, I was immensely grateful to have the support and care of others.

In reading the brief exchange between Koestler and Grey I got the impression that there was a great deal more both of them could say about the subject. In referring to 'talking away' the experience of solitude, Koestler suggested that it could be that he was attempting to preserve the experience by being deliberately reticent. They both indicated that solitary confinement was for them a kind of mystical experience. 'You have a feeling of inner freedom. Of being alone and confronted with inner realities . . . So you have got a dialogue with life, a dialogue with death,' wrote Koestler. That statement, I believe, begins to touch the essence of the experience. In prolonged solitude there is the possibility of facing realities that are indeed difficult to express verbally. It is a though we confront, within ourselves, the mighty forces that shape the universe, and in the face of such forces we are rendered silent. We are both repelled and attracted at the same moment. Attracted by the mystery of the experience and repelled by the power that we realize has the capacity to swallow us, as a black hole might swallow light.

It was in the face of such an experience that symbols took on a great significance for me. Koestler comments: 'Whether it is the cross or the crescent moon or the shield of David, they are symbols, man made symbols for a reality that cannot be formulated.' I made a simple cross from toilet paper, and each day I saved a small piece of bread so that I could begin the day by celebrating Holy Communion. I intuitively realized that both the symbols and the symbolic action would somehow relate me to an experience that was too deep for me to verbalize. Now that I am some years away from the experience of complete solitude, I have become increasingly frustrated with the verbosity present within certain religious services. I am increasingly attracted by the silence of the Quakers and the symbolic expressions of the Orthodox, which provide a background for the intensity of a solitary encounter. For those who have no experience of participating in an Orthodox liturgy, I should explain that the drama of the event is enacted by the celebrants, as they follow an elaborate ritual. Members of the congregation are free to follow their own devotions within the context of an all-embracing event. Anglicanism, and to a certain extent Roman Catholicism, has been active in recent years in diminishing symbolic language in favour of extempore prayers and contemporary language, and has almost become obsessed with getting the congregation to 'respond' or 'participate'. In many such churches today it is virtually impossible for an individual to be solitary within the context of community worship. That is not true of the other two religious groups I have mentioned.

During solitary confinement I became increasingly aware of my own mortality, not only because I was actually facing severe threats due to the uncertain temperament of my captors and was at times kept in locations that were under shellfire, but because of the nature of the experience itself. I was driven to a level of introspection that was both frightening and rewarding. Once again I turn to the words of Koestler who, in a broadcast on the BBC Third Programme in 1960, said:

> You no doubt remember your old sage who said that philosophy is the history of man's endeavours to come to terms with death. And since

philosophy is a good thing, death must be a good thing – or at least awareness thereof. Take the word 'death' out of your vocabulary and your great works of literature become meaningless; take the awareness away and your cathedrals collapse, the pyramids vanish into the sand and the great organs become silent. You know all this but since you live in an age of anxiety and transition, you condemn all concerns with death as morbid in the indignant voice of your Victorian prudes. You deny Thanatos as the Victorians denied Eros; you shrink from the facts of death as they shrank from the facts of life. And yet the philosophy of man, the art of man, the dignity of man is derived from his brave endeavours to reconcile Eros with Thanatos.

Experiencing years of solitary life is, as already indicated, difficult to explain. I have compared it to crossing a vast desert. For day after day you plod onwards with your eyes fixed on the horizon, looking for an end to the ordeal. As the days, months, years pass by, time takes on a new meaning. Instead of always looking to the far distance, you begin to look around and discover that far from being a bleak and arid place the desert is teeming with life. The journey is indeed exhausting, but gradually you learn to live for the moment. You begin to mark the route with symbolic expressions that extend beyond the limitations of time: a paper cross, symbolic language. The world you thought was beyond the horizon is also within you and all around. Death now no longer lies over the horizon. Now Thanatos (the Greek personification of death) has become a companion who walks alongside without threat. Within the relationship you have with him is an inexpressible sadness that comes from the knowledge that death is certainly the one encounter in life that we must face alone. Death, whom we have tried to keep at a distance and ignore, has always been at our side. Now we have eyes to see him, and the conversation with him is what we make it. We can remain fixed on the horizon and attempt to escape the reality of the moment, or we can enter into a relationship that opens up new dimensions for us in life. Rather than being depressed by the reality of human existence we can be stimulated by the relationship that opens up the possibility of being invigorated by the experience.

The two former members of the Intelligence Service that I wrote about earlier (now dead) both made one simple point. They accommodated themselves to living a lie. No one can afford to be sanctimonious about this as, to a greater or lesser extent, we all fail to walk totally in the light. They were able to live a lie because they believed that by acting they did they were working for the greater good of their country. This is not the place to discuss this moral point, but it is certainly well worth discussing further. Ted, who had led such a colourful life as an agent, was, when I met him, experiencing the solitude of the carer as, day after day, he gave attention to his ailing partner. That is a form of solitude known to thousands of people and not infrequently leads to a further experience – the solitude of grief.

A comparatively short, but valuable, conversation in this book took place with the matron of a hospice, who had just retired. For me the main point that stood out in the interview was that the matron did not regard death as an enemy to be defeated at any cost. It was an inevitable part of life that would come to us all sooner or later, and a part of her job had been to enable her patients to face it with dignity and composure.

I have stood on the edge of life several times, and one of the closest times I came to crossing the threshold was when I faced a mock execution in Beirut. Although I was afraid, my fear was not of death itself but of whether or not it would hurt when the bullet went through me. I recollect a deep calmness and an experience that seemed to lift me out of the squalid situation I was in, to a point outside myself. Once again I find it difficult, if not impossible, to convey that experience in words.

*

My reflections on solitude would not be complete (not that they could ever be totally complete) without some observations on the dark side of my own experience of it following captivity. Although I would not class myself as a depressive, like most people there are times when darkness takes the upper hand for a couple of days and almost overwhelms me. When that happens, it is extremely difficult to shake off and the more close friends try to help, the deeper I sink into the darkness. How does one begin to explain such an experience?

It can be triggered by a seemingly innocent upset – let us say the postponement of something that I was greatly looking forward to. The trigger is trivial in itself and normally would be dismissed. However, something takes place deep within, which drives me deeper and deeper into despair. I long for the company of others and yet cannot bear it when it is offered. My surroundings may be idyllic, but they provide no comfort. Rather they seem to increase the feeling of isolation and despair. In the midst of this encompassing darkness, aggressive feelings rk. There is the temptation to tear up what I have written. It seems worthless. (I have resisted that temptation, but I can hear some readers say, 'Pity you didn't!') Mercifully I have never experienced the desire to self-harm or to hurt others physically. I suspect I give way sometimes to the impulse to hurt others emotionally, but there is no long-term satisfaction in that. There is little to be done, apart from sitting out the experience and waiting for the cloud to lift, which in my case it does within a couple of days. These attacks of depression are mercifully few and far between, but when they do strike, they strike with a force that renders me virtually helpless. I am fortunate in that I have never suffered from nightmares or flashbacks to my captivity. In fact, I continue to experience what I experienced then: my dreams are often interesting and frequently funny. They provide some escape from the bleakness of the waking hours.

I need to balance what I have written by saying that the experience itself has not proved to be totally negative. Once the mood has passed I get a surge of creativity. Writing, which during the darkness was impossible, becomes a joy. Music, which was deadening and virtually unbearable, once again breathes a language of harmony. I believe that the infrequent attacks that have occurred since I was released are reflecting, in some measure, the deep isolation experienced thirty years ago. Religious individuals might describe this experience as the dark night of the soul. However it is described, it is painful, but it has not destroyed me.

*

Alas, I lost contact with Bruce Farrands and his wife some years ago and when I came to write this book I looked up Rabbit Flat on the internet. According to what I read, Jacqui was injured by a drunken traveller and Bruce suffered some form of accident. It was then, in 2010, that they decided to call it a day and moved away to be near their son in Queensland. They were a remarkable couple and although the picture painted of Bruce by some of the internet commentators portrays a bad-tempered old man, that is certainly not my recollection of him. He was direct and outspoken, to be sure, and he had a passionate dislike of bureaucracy, but he was none the worse for that. Over the years they had both developed a remarkable resilience to the many difficulties that faced them in their isolated home, but they were content. At least that is the impression they gave me. To a large extent they lived a self-contained life broken only by passing travellers, although at times that life was totally disrupted by drunken disturbances. I often wonder how they have adapted to life in a very different environment.

One of the most obviously contented people I met on this journey through solitude was Terry Underwood, at the Riveren Station, six hundred miles south-west of Katherine, Australia. She spoke eloquently about her life and seemed to me to be a wonderfully rounded individual. Some years ago she published a book entitled *In the Middle of Nowhere*, which portrays life in the remote outback. In remote locations it is necessary to create your own world, and both Terry and Bruce had been able to do that and find contentment.

For many years I have been associated with the Emmaus movement in the UK. Emmaus is an organization that was founded in France following the Second World War by the late Abbé Pierre and came to the UK some twenty-five years ago. In a most creative way, it enables homeless people (mainly single homeless, but not exclusively so) to enter into a community and begin to live life as fully as they are capable of. My conversations with Sammy in Chicago, and to a lesser extent with Ronnie in Australia, reminded me of the many people I have met in Emmaus over the years. In so many cases they have had, through no fault of their own, a very difficult childhood and a lifetime littered with misfortune of one kind or another. Many individuals who eventually discover an Emmaus community have spent years living a solitary existence, walking the streets and sleeping under market stalls. Understandably, so many of them have very low self-esteem. By providing each individual who enters an Emmaus community with a room of their own, it gives them the opportunity to have their own space, their own privacy. By working alongside other community members, they are gradually reconciled to living in community and living life to capacity. Sammy seemed to me to represent the thousands of lonely people living in isolation in our cities. In days past, and to a certain extent today in smaller communities, such individuals are recognized and in varying ways supported. In our vast conurbations they become lost souls. Ronnie, living with his little dog Misty in the Australian outback, had throughout his life accommodated himself to the solitary life and in his old age found reasonable contentment.

By no means would I regard this book as a full examination of the solitary experience. Rather, I have attempted to present a series of snapshots that give some insight into the solitary life as experienced in a variety of circumstances. I cannot do better than to close with a quotation from *Letters to a Young Poet* by Rainer Maria Rilke:

Postlude

Love your solitude and try to sing out with the pain it causes you. For those who are near you are far away . . . and this shows that the space around you is beginning to grow vast . . . be happy about your growth, in which of course you can't take anyone with you, and be gentle with those who stay behind; be confident and calm in front of them and don't torment them with your doubts and don't frighten them with your faith or joy, which they wouldn't be able to comprehend. Seek out some simple and true feeling of what you have in common with them, which doesn't necessarily have to alter when you yourself change again and again; when you see them, love life in a form that is not your own and be indulgent toward those who are growing old, who are afraid of the aloneness that you trust . . . and don't expect any understanding; but believe in a love that is being stored up for you like an inheritance, and have faith that in this love there is a strength and a blessing so large that you can travel as far as you wish without having to step outside it.